Bird-Friendly
Nest Boxes & Feeders

12 Easy-to-Build Designs That Attract Birds to Your Yard

Bird-Friendly
Nest Boxes & Feeders

12 Easy-to-Build Designs That Attract Birds to Your Yard

PAUL MEISEL

FOX CHAPEL
PUBLISHING

Thanks to the following people for the bird photos on pages 106 and 107:
American robin, photo © Laura Erickson
House finch, titmouse, and Carolina wren, public domain photos
    by www.kenthomas.us
American kestrel, photo by Jurvetson (flickr)*
Northern saw-whet owl, barn swallow, and tree swallow, photos
    by Brendan Lally (flikr: brendan.lally)*
Least flycatcher, photo by Seabamirum (flikr)*
White-breasted nuthatch and yellow warbler, photos
    by Pierre Bonenfant (flikr: pbonenfant)*
Eastern phoebe, photo by John Benson (flikr: ibm4381)*
* Photos used under the terms of the CC-BY license:
    (http://creativecommons.org/licenses/by /3.0/legalcode)

ISBN 978-1-56523-692-9

Library of Congress Cataloging-in-Publication Data

Meisel, Paul, 1946-
 Bird-friendly nest boxes and feeders / Paul Meisel.
    p. cm.
 Includes index.
 ISBN 978-1-56523-692-9
 1. Birdhouses--Design and construction. 2. Bird feeders--Design and construction. I. Title.
 QL676.5.M379 2012
 728.927--dc23
                              2011039673

To learn more about the other great books from Fox Chapel Publishing, or to find a retailer near you, call toll-free 800-457-9112 or visit us at *www.FoxChapelPublishing.com*.

Note to Authors: We are always looking for talented authors to write new books in our area of woodworking, design, and related crafts. Please send a brief letter describing your idea to Acquisition Editor, 1970 Broad Street, East Petersburg, PA 17520.

Printed in China
First printing
Second printing

Dedication

I would like to dedicate this book to Roger Strand for his work helping to restore wood duck populations and to Andrew Troyer for his work helping to restore purple martin and bluebird populations.

Acknowledgements

Thanks to Boyd Emerson, Kim Truax, and Johanna Rich for help building, designing, and photographing the projects. Thanks to Lorrie Ham for help proofing the manuscript. Thanks to Andrew Troyer for allowing me to incorporate his bluebird house design. Thanks to Diane Oberlander and John Nisley for providing photographs for the Bluebird House project. Thanks to Dr. Joseph Valks for use of the photograph of the starling. Thanks to Roger Strand of the Wood Duck Society for providing photographs for the Wood Duck House and for sharing his expertise in mounting wood duck houses according to his Best Practices method. Thanks to Jeff Ratcliff for use of the photograph of the sparrow. Thanks to John Wagman for his design of the Martin House.

Learn to make birdhouses and feeders that...

...are designed to aid in the recovery of endangered or threatened bird species.

...discourage unwelcome visitors like squirrels, sparrows, and starlings.

...allow for easy inspection and cleaning.

...invite wonderful bird species into your backyard.

Contents

Birdhouses:

Bird Feeders:

Introduction

No matter where you live, placing birdhouses and feeders outside your home will give you a front-row seat to a fun and nature-oriented pastime: watching the antics of wild birds. Watching birds attend to their newborns and witnessing the first awkward flights as a new generation learns how to fly is most rewarding. It's also a great way to promote the survival of wild bird populations.

Different birds prefer different feeders and styles of nestboxes. The projects in this book are designed to give you lots of options, and none of them require specialized tools. If you know basic construction techniques (covered on pages 16–19) and have access to a basic home workshop with a table saw, scroll saw, drill press, and common hand tools, you can make these projects. A router and a drum sander (or a drum sander attachment for a drill press) are helpful but not necessary. The building materials—exterior plywood or pine or cedar boards—are readily available from home centers or lumberyards.

Getting the Tenants You Want

About 30 different species of birds are known to nest in birdhouses. Most will be welcome visitors to your yard, but a few are not as desirable. Among those few are the starling and the house sparrow, found in all forty-eight continental states, and the song sparrow, found in the northern half of the United States.

Both sparrows and starlings will build nests almost anywhere, showing little preference as to cavity size, height, or location—over doors or windows, on ledges, or in tree cavities. Sparrows stuff all manner of nest-building material through the entrance opening, almost always leaving some unsightly pieces of string, grass, or other debris hanging from a birdhouse's entrance hole.

Sparrows steal food from other species, including native American songbirds. On the bright side, sparrows do have a cheerful chirp and, like other birds, eat many harmful insects. Starlings are also aggressive, traveling in large flocks that may literally take over an area's food and shelter. Like bullies, they drive out other species of birds or, worse yet, kill them with their sharp bills.

Although they will build nests just about anywhere, in birdhouses sparrows and starlings prefer a 1½" (38mm)-diameter hole. You can try to deter them by making your birdhouse's hole smaller than that, but that may also discourage other bird species. Starlings typically don't enter birdhouses with entrances less than 1½" (38mm) in diameter, but sparrows will try to use any birdhouse except one with a tiny hole just big enough for wrens.

The aggressive starling, introduced from England, is considered a menace to domestic United States birds.

The common house sparrow, introduced from England, now competes with North American song birds for available food and housing.

MODIFYING PLANS

One of the joys of making projects from wood is that, with a little ingenuity, you can sometimes modify a project slightly to accommodate a particular species of bird. Appendix C (page 106) lists dimensions likely to attract a variety of bird species. By enlarging or reducing the size of the birdhouse or the entrance hole diameter, you can modify some of the birdhouses in this book to more closely match the preferences of various birds.

For example, house wrens, brown-throated wrens, and Bewick's wrens nest in houses with a 1" (25mm)-diameter hole. Chickadees nest in houses with a 1⅛" (29mm)-diameter hole. Birds that prefer a 1¼" (32mm)-diameter hole include the nuthatch, downy woodpecker, and titmouse. Some birds, including tree swallows and warblers, prefer a 1½" (38mm)-diameter hole, as do sparrows and starlings.

Remember that for thousands of years, birds have successfully searched out nesting locations in the wild. Cavities left by woodpeckers or holes in rotted tree branches are among the choices available. Seldom do these natural cavities match precisely the cavity size and entrance hole diameter listed in Appendix C. However, the suggested dimensions are valuable because experimentation has shown that wild birds are *more likely* to nest in man-made houses matching the given dimensions. That said, you will never know which species might decide to move in. Part of the joy of providing bird feeders and birdhouses is waiting to see which birds select your yard as a feeding ground or as a building location for their nests and place to raise their young.

Picking the Right Feeder

There are three main varieties of bird feeders: Ground feeders, hanging feeders, and post-mounted feeders.

Ground feeders may be just a piece of wood raised a few feet off the ground with seeds thrown on top of it. I have not included any of these, because they tend to attract birds that eat seed from the ground, including many less desirable species such as sparrows, grackles, and starlings, as well as mice and other rodents. Additionally, the seeds in ground feeders are susceptible to rot and mold when it rains.

Hanging feeders are typically suspended from a tree branch or an overhead support. Although most of the feeders in this book can be hung, it is not necessarily the best mounting method. Wind tends to make hanging feeders swing, which can be quite unsettling to some bird species. Birds such as nuthatches, chickadees, and finches, however, will have no trouble feeding from a hanging feeder.

Attaching your feeder or birdhouse to a stationary post is the preferred mounting method for several reasons. You can place the post anywhere, it eliminates wind swinging, and you can adjust the height so it is

A ½" (13mm) pipe with a floor flange holds smaller birdhouses and bird feeders. Use ¾" (19mm) pipe for larger projects. Remember pipe is measured on the inside diameter.

within your reach, which simplifies refilling. The post also provides a place to attach a squirrel baffle, and is especially suited to supporting heavy feeders. Steel pipe, sometimes sold as water or gas pipe, is not expensive and is available in most hardware stores. A floor flange can be threaded on the end of the pipe to make an easy attachment point for the feeder. To remove the feeder for cleaning, simply unscrew the floor flange from the post.

Getting Started

Now that you know more about birdhouses and feeders, it's time to introduce you to some of the tools and methods you'll need to complete the projects in this book. Read on to learn how you can reduce the effects of the environment on your finished projects and review the sample project to get a handle on the woodworking methods you'll need to know.

Understanding the Projects

Each project is composed of the same elements. For every project you will find:

1. A photograph and description of the project

2. How-To Instructions;

3. Final Assembly instructions and exploded Assembly Drawings;

4. A Bill of Materials listing the size of all wood materials as well as any hardware required; and

5. Finishing suggestions.

Each element helps you gain an understanding of the project you wish to undertake, so you can easily and quickly finish it and begin enjoying your feathered friends.

COLOR PHOTOGRAPH AND DESCRIPTION

The color picture introducing each project gives you a good idea of what the finished product will look like, especially if you use the same type of wood and the same stain or paint colors suggested. Read over the description to learn background information about the project. This can help you decide which project to make first, or which one is right for your yard.

TIP: The various tips presented throughout this book provide some valuable information on how to attract birds to your yard, which seeds attract which species, how to store birdseed safely, and which birdhouse sizes are appropriate for certain birds. There are even suggestions for painting and finishing your projects. Take time to page through the book and see what you can learn.

HOW-TO INSTRUCTIONS

The How-To Instructions describe how to proceed with the cutting of each piece of wood needed to build the project. For scroll-shaped pieces that would typically be cut on a scroll saw or band saw, transfer the pattern to the wood, then saw out the part. Large plan sheets that include full-size plans are available and can be purchased separately for each project in this book. See the ordering information in Appendix A (page 104).

For square- or rectangular-shaped parts best cut on a table saw, the How-To Instructions say, "Lay out and cut to size." Do this by setting your table saw to rip the board to width or crosscut it to length. Where angles are required or where holes need to be drilled, use layout tools to mark these locations on your wood.

If two or more identical pieces are required, it will be noted in the How-To Instructions (i.e., two pieces required).

FINAL ASSEMBLY INSTRUCTIONS AND EXPLODED DRAWINGS

Once you have cut each piece to size, it is time to assemble the parts. The Final Assembly instructions, together with the exploded assembly drawings, describe how the pieces of the project fit together and the order in which to assemble them. Refer to both when assembling the project.

Although the assembly sequence is explained, the choice of fasteners is left, for the most part, to the preferences of the builder. For general construction, either nails or screws can be used. On critical joints where screws should be used for strength, the screw-hole locations are shown on the plan drawings and the recommended screw size are given in the Bill of Materials. Be sure to use water-resistant glue for all glue joints. Use nails or screws designed for exterior use.

Remember that birdhouses and feeders must be periodically cleaned. Birdhouses typically feature a removable top, bottom, or side for this purpose. For feeders with an enclosed hopper, the top or top section is made to be removable. For this reason, screws (no glue) are used to facilitate partially disassembling most of the projects in this book.

For birdhouses with an inset bottom that must be removed for cleaning, remember to cut the bottom slightly undersized so it won't fit too tightly.

Although not included on the drawings themselves, ventilation holes should be drilled at the top of every birdhouse. Birdhouses stationed in hotter climates require larger vent holes than those in cooler climates. Although not shown on the plans, the top of the left and right sides of some birdhouses can be shortened by ¼" (6mm) to allow increased side-to-side ventilation.

Drainage holes should be drilled in the floors of all birdhouses. Drill four or more drainage holes through the floor using a ¼" (6mm)-diameter or larger bit. Another method is to nib the corners of the floor at 45 degrees.

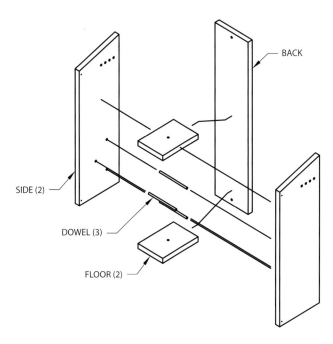

BACK

SIDE (2)

DOWEL (3)

FLOOR (2)

BILL OF MATERIALS

A Bill of Materials list is provided for each plan and contains a great deal of information. The first column indicates the number of pieces required, the second column provides a description, and the last column shows the size. Wood parts are listed by thickness, width, and length, with the smallest piece at the top of the Bill of Materials.

Required hardware parts are listed together with a description and size. Nails and wood dowels should be easy for you to purchase locally. Other hardware items such as plastic side plates, hinges, hooks, flush mount-hangers, and plastic plugs can sometimes be found in hardware stores, but should you have difficulty locating them, they are available for mail order from Meisel Hardware Specialties.

In a few cases I have omitted drawing simple square- or rectangular-shaped parts. In these instances, "not drawn" appears in parentheses after that part. Simply cut these parts to the widths and lengths given.

Finishes to Protect Your Projects Outdoors

Cedar is a very hardy wood that does not need a finish to look good and perform well outdoors. If you wish to use a finish on cedar projects, I recommend sanding sealer followed by a coat of exterior polyurethane.

Pine and exterior plywood don't handle the harsh outdoor environment nearly as well as cedar does, so they should always be painted or finished with some type of exterior stain or other exterior finish. If you choose paint, it is important to use the highest quality primer and paint available—exterior house paint is a good choice. You could even make your birdhouse match your house.

The harsh effects of outdoor weather are very damaging to wood and paint. The three biggest culprits are ultraviolet (UV) radiation, particularly from direct sunlight, which makes paint lose its color and break down into white, chalky dust; moisture, which causes the same paint problems that UV radiation does, plus blistering as the underlying wood swells and contracts; and changes in temperature, which are much greater than they are indoors, and cause wood to expand and contract, particularly stressing paint. All grades of paint suffer these effects to some degree, but low-quality paints and interior paints generally fail earlier than top-quality exterior paints.

STAIN-BLOCKING PRIMERS

A primer is a paint coating designed to form a film on which a succeeding finish coat, or coats, of paint can be applied.

If painting your project, begin by covering all knots and other wood defects with a stain-blocking primer to avoid bleed-through, a brownish or tan discoloration that appears sometimes several months after the project has been painted. Stain bleed-through looks particularly unsightly on white or light-colored paints. William Zinsser & Company, Inc. and Masterchem Industries, LLC manufacture popular stain-blocking primers.

Next, prime the entire project. You could also use the stain-blocking primer for that, but I prefer to use a white exterior acrylic latex primer because it is thinner and therefore soaks into the wood better. After priming, sand with 220-grit sandpaper and begin painting the various colors of the topcoats.

TIP: Never attempt to paint wood that has high moisture content. Allow wet wood to dry first.

ACRYLIC LATEX PAINT VERSUS OIL-BASED PAINT

Acrylic latex primers and gloss or semi-gloss acrylic latex exterior paints are the best choice for outdoor wood projects. This is not to say that oil-based primers and paints should not be used. Oil-based primers do have their advantages. For example, they are better suited to hide imperfections and therefore have better coverage. They also offer better adhesion to wood and therefore seal the surface better. However, after considerable experimenting, I have found acrylic latex primer and paint to be the all-around best choice for painting outdoor projects.

While the binders in oil paints (particularly in red and yellow colors) absorb UV radiation, often breaking down as a result, acrylic latex paint binders tend to be transparent to radiation and so fare better. Where moisture or temperature swings cause wood to swell and contract, acrylic latex paint also does better than oil paints because it is permeable, allowing the water to vaporize and escape, and offers superior adhesion and flexibility that resist cracking and flaking. Top-quality acrylic latex paint is an especially good choice for exterior applications in areas where there are many heavy freeze/thaw cycles.

The chart below outlines some additional advantages of acrylic latex paints versus oil-based paints.

When you purchase paints, be sure to have your dealer shake them. This ensures all the pigment is suspended evenly throughout the paint. Also be sure to ask the paint dealer for complimentary wooden stir sticks. Use these wood sticks to mix the paint immediately after opening the can and periodically while you are painting to be absolutely sure the color and pigment stay evenly distributed.

Don't apply extra-heavy coats of either primer or paint. An extra-heavy coat does not necessarily offer better protection. In fact, coats that are too thick will probably crack, resulting in less protection.

	Acrylic latex	Oil-based
Drying time	1–4 hours	24–48 hours
Vehicle	Non-flammable; minimal offensive odor	Flammable; toxic, mineral-based
Fumes	Minimal risk of inhalation	Toxic; if used indoors, must be well ventilated
Liquid used for thinning	Water	Paint thinner or turpentine
Cleanup	Warm water & soap	Paint thinner or turpentine (must be well ventilated)

Examples of stain-blocking primers available in most hardware stores and home centers.

Constructing a Nest Box—A Sample Project

Building a nest box requires not only wood and tools, but also some personal experience using those tools. In other words, it requires a certain amount of woodworking skill. Simple nest boxes like the small raptor house require a minimum of skill and can be accomplished by almost any hobbyist. Here is a sample project that provides some practical information hobbyists of any skill level should find helpful. Although it pertains to the small raptor box, much of the information applies to other projects in this book.

TOOLS AND MATERIALS

Here is a list of the tools and materials required to build the small raptor nest box. The tools and materials for other projects in this book will vary.

Tools:

- Table saw
- Hand drill or a drill press
- Drill bits of various sizes
- 3" (76mm) Forstner bit to drill the entrance hole (A jig saw or scroll saw can be substituted.)
- 16 oz. (454g.) claw hammer
- Scratch awl
- Ruler or steel measuring tape
- Square
- ¾" (19mm) spindle sander or round file
- #2 Philips-head screwdriver
- Lead pencil

Materials:

- 1" x 10" (25 x 254mm) pine boards
- 1½" x 1½" (38 x 38mm) hinge
- Masking tape
- Water-resistant adhesive
- Casing nails or wood screws
- Screen-door hook
- Exterior primer and paint

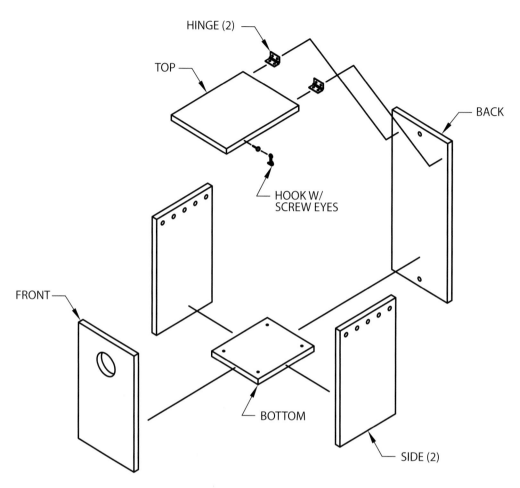

HINGE (2)

TOP

BACK

HOOK W/
SCREW EYES

FRONT

BOTTOM

SIDE (2)

ASSEMBLY DRAWING

Bill of Materials

Qty.	Part	Size of Material
1	Bottom	¾" x 7¾" x 9¼" (19 x 197 x 235mm)
1	Top	¾" x 9¼" x 12" (19 x 235 x 305mm)
1	Front	¾" x 9¼" x 16" (19 x 235 x 406mm)
2	Side	¾" x 9¼" x 16" (19 x 235 x 406mm)
1	Back	¾" x 9¼" x 22" (19 x 235 x 559mm)
1 pair	Hinge	
2	Hook w/ Screw Eye	

Each project in this book contains a Cutting Diagram showing how much wood to purchase. The amount of lumber required depends to some degree on the number of knots, stains, splits, and other defects you have to cut around. Some defects, such as small, tight knots, may not affect the strength or usefulness of the lumber. If, however, your lumber contains large or loose knots, cracks, splits, or other severe defects, you'll need to cut around these problem areas. The illustration below shows the Cutting Diagram for the small raptor nest box. Although the purpose of the Cutting Diagram is to show how much lumber will be needed, these diagrams do not take into account the fact that lumber usually has some defects (i.e., unusable areas that must be cut around and discarded). The illustration shows a defect-free 1" x 10" x 96" (25 x 254 x 2438mm) board, but in the photo below, you can see the parts were arranged to take the best advantage of the defect-free parts of the lumber. In this case, two boards were necessary for all of the parts. (There was some unused lumber on the right end of the bottom board.)

1" X 10" X 8'

CUTTING DIAGRAM

Cut the individual pieces to width and length. As described in the Introduction (page 8), the How-To Instructions lists each piece of the project and how to cut and prepare each piece.

SIDE | WASTE | FLOOR | WASTE | SIDE | WASTE | TOP
FRONT | WASTE | BACK | (UNUSED)

Assemble the cut pieces. Once the individual pieces of the project have been cut to size, determine the type of fastener you wish to use to assemble the project. Any fastener you choose should be rust resistant. The nail and screw in the photo at left are galvanized—coated with a protective layer of zinc. Zinc can either be electroplated onto the fastener or be applied using a process called hot dipping. Electroplating leaves only a thin, smooth coat of metal. Electroplated coatings in various metals used on screws prevent rusting. Nails with a smooth finish may loosen over time. This is not an issue with screws. If available, choose nails that have been hot dipped. In the hot dipping process, the nails are dropped into liquid zinc, which results in a much thicker and rougher surface texture. These nails hold extremely well. The 2" (51mm)-long (6 penny) casing nail in the photo at left was used to assemble the small raptor house. The #6 gauge 2" (51mm)-long steel screw in the photo was finished with electroplated metal followed by a coating of clear plastic. These fasteners are excellent choices for assembling the raptor nest box.

Mark holes for the fasteners. With a ruler and sharp lead pencil, mark the locations of the fasteners. For the small raptor nest box, four nails were used on each side of the front piece, and two fasteners were used on the bottom of the front piece. Mark the locations of these holes with a scratch awl.

Pre-drill holes for the fasteners. Whether you use nails or screws, it is a good idea to pre-drill the holes for the fasteners. For nails, drill holes slightly smaller that the diameter of the nail you are using. For screws, drill "clearance" holes in the top piece of wood that are as close as possible to the outside diameter of the screw threads. Drill smaller "pilot" holes in the piece to which the first board is to be attached. Pre-drill any other holes such as the two ½" (13mm) attachment holes on the top and bottom of the back piece and the 3" (76mm) entrance hole on the front piece. In the photo above, holes for nails are being drilled in the front piece of the small raptor nest box.

Apply glue. Run a bead of water-resistant glue around those parts you'll be fastening together. Here, the sides have already been attached to the bottom piece. The box is being readied so the front piece can be nailed on.

Nail the parts. After the sides are glued and nailed to the bottom, the front is nailed on, and then the back.

Attach the top. The top of the small raptor nest box is attached with a pair of hinges. Position the top, place the hinges about 1" (25mm) in from each side and mark the screw hole locations with a sharp lead pencil. Next, mark the screw hole positions with a scratch awl.

Drill the hinge screw pilot holes. To prevent accidentally drilling all the way through your wood, wrap a piece of masking tape ⅝" (16mm) from the end of the bit to act as a depth gauge.

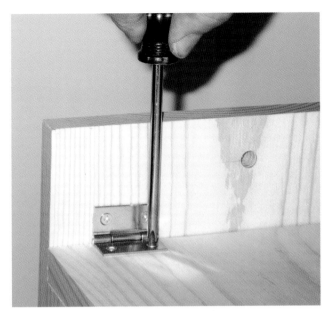

Install the hinges. Install the hinges with a #2 Phillips-head screwdriver.

Drill ventilation holes. Use a ½" bit to drill air ventilation holes in the side pieces.

Install the screen-door hook. Place a screen-door hook on one or both sides to hold the top securely closed. Adjust the hook so it is tight enough that predators such as raccoons can't open it and eat the eggs or the nestlings.

The beautiful bluebird, with its blue and red plumage, is part of the thrush family.

POSITION OF CEILING

Bluebird House

Many people consider bluebirds their favorite songbird. Besides their beautiful song, these birds have a disposition that, by their very presence, makes people feel good. They are gentle, inquisitive, and just plain fun to watch. These pleasant creatures with their blue and red plumage are from the thrush family. The bluebird is the state bird of both Missouri and New York, while the mountain bluebird is the state bird of Idaho.

If you haven't seen any bluebirds recently, it may be the result of an enormous loss of their habitat due to factors like redevelopment and reforestation of farmlands. In addition, many have been killed by pesticides and herbicides. To make matters worse, the proliferation of sparrows and starlings, both non-native species introduced from Europe, compete with bluebirds for available nesting sites. Both sparrows and starlings are known to destroy bluebird eggs and kill both baby and adult bluebirds.

By the 1970s, bluebird populations had declined drastically, up to 70 percent by some estimates. The good news is that counts have been increasing in large part because of a movement by volunteers to establish and maintain multiple bluebird houses, referred to as bluebird trails.

Andrew Troyer of Conneautville, Pennsylvania, developed the design of this bluebird house. It incorporates all the most desirable features for attracting bluebirds. The horizontal entry hole discourages sparrows from entering the house and killing the bluebirds. The front of the box opens easily to monitor the eggs and nestlings.

The house can be built from standard lumber sizes, and the design has been approved by bluebird organizations like the Bluebird Recovery Program of Minnesota.

Through periodic inspections you can record the number of eggs in a brood and monitor the progress of the baby birds, checking for problems like insect infestations. (Bluebirds have a poor sense of smell and so are not bothered by human scent.)

An Internet search of bluebird monitoring provides a great deal of information on monitoring, recording observations, and where to report this information once you have gathered it.

How-To Instructions

This bluebird house can be made from a short length of 2x4 (38 x 89mm) and a 1x10 (19 x 235mm) board. The amount of material you will need is shown in the Cutting Diagram.

Hinge the Front at the bottom on two nails. Latch the top of the Front piece with a loose pin, which can be a nail that is bent, as shown on Step 2 of the Assembly Drawing. This pin can be placed on one or both sides.

By pulling the pin(s), the Front of the house can be swung open to examine the inside cavity. The holes for the pins are called out in the drawing of the Side piece as being ¹⁄₁₆" (2mm). This size varies depending on the diameter of the nail. The holes in the Side pieces should be slightly larger than the diameter of the nails. The nail holes in the bottom of the Front piece should be pre-drilled with a bit smaller than the diameter of the nail. Slip the two nails used to hinge the Front through the lower holes in the Side pieces and then pound them

into the Front piece. The loose pin(s) at the top should be easy to pull out and remove. Drill the hole(s) through the outside of the Side piece and into the top of the Front piece. The holes must be slightly larger than the diameter of the nail.

Make saw cuts around all four edges of the bottom surface of the Roof. The purpose of the saw cuts is to prevent rainwater from creeping under the Roof and working its way to the inside of the house.

The Tray piece holds wood shavings. It is not permanently attached to the inside of the house, so it can be removed easily for cleaning. Use a 2³⁄₈" (60mm)-diameter Forstner bit for drilling the hole in the Tray piece.

Begin by cutting each of the parts as described below. Then assemble the project according to the Final Assembly instructions and as shown in the Assembly Drawing.

The front of the box opens easily, so you can clean the birdhouse or monitor the nestlings.

Use a horizontal entrance hole to keep sparrows out of your birdhouse. Note the numbers at the base of the house. This numbering system is utilized to keep records of the multiple houses on a "bluebird trail."

TIP: Never install a perch below the entrance hole on the front of any birdhouse. The perch offers starlings, house sparrows, and other predators a convenient place to wait for lunch. Perches do nothing but help predators kill the birds you are trying to protect.

FLOOR AND FRONT: Lay out and cut to size from ¾" (19mm) stock. Cut the 15-degree bevel.

CEILING: Lay out and cut to size from ¾" (19mm) stock.

SIDE: Lay out and cut to size from ¾" (19mm) stock. Drill the ¹⁄₁₆" (2mm)-diameter and ¼" (6mm)-diameter holes through (Two pieces required).

ROOF: Lay out and cut to size from ¾" (19mm) stock. Cut the ⅛"-wide-by-⅛"-deep (3 x 3mm) grooves.

GUSSET: Lay out and cut to size from 1½" (38mm) stock. Cut the 45-degree bevel.

TRAY: Lay out and cut to size from 1½" (38mm) stock. Cut the 15-degree bevel. Drill the 2⅜" (60mm)-diameter hole 1" (25mm) deep.

BACK: Lay out and cut to size from 1½" (38mm) stock.

FINAL ASSEMBLY

STEP 1: Attach the Sides to the Back. Attach the Gusset to the Ceiling. Attach the Floor and Ceiling to the Sides.

STEP 2: Place the Front piece between the Side pieces in the position shown on the drawing of the Side piece. The top of the Front piece should be from 1³⁄₁₆" to 1¼" (30 to 32mm) from the bottom of the Ceiling piece. It is called out at 1¼" (32mm) on the drawing of the Side piece. Drive two 2¼" (57mm) nails through the bottom holes in the Side piece and into the Front piece to act as a hinge. Insert bent 2¼" (57mm) nail(s) in the top to act as a latch. Aluminum pop rivets can be substituted for the bent nails. Nail the Roof to the Ceiling where shown. Place the Tray on the Floor piece. Do not attach the Tray, as it should be removable for cleaning. Fill the Tray with nesting material such as wood shavings.

Bluebird houses should be mounted on a steel post. Choose a length of 1" (25mm) steel electrical conduit, ¾" (19mm) galvanized water pipe (remember, pipe is measured using the inside diameter), or a steel fence post. If using round tubing or pipe, be sure the house is attached securely and does not rotate. U-bolts work well for attaching the birdhouse to a round pipe. If using a steel fence post, attach the house with hanger strap, which is made from steel and should be available at any hardware store. It is sold in a roll, generally about ¾" (19mm) wide. Holes are punched about every half-inch (13mm) along the length. Cut two pieces long enough to bend around the post and extend to the width of the 2x4 (38 x 89mm) Back. Secure each end with a wood screw. Two straps are sufficient to secure a house to a fence post.

The best post length is 8' (2438mm). You can bury 2' (610mm) in the ground and mount the house at approximately eye level, making it easy to inspect. This height also keeps most cats from jumping up from the ground and eating the birds. Attaching a predator guard on the fence post just below the house is strongly recommended. (A source for purchasing predator guards is listed in the Resources section of this book.) This prevents raccoons, snakes, and squirrels from reaching the house. Bluebird houses should be placed in open land with low ground cover. They like the mowed grass around golf courses. Keep bluebird houses at least 100' (30m) from the tree line to discourage house wrens from competing for the house (house wrens tend not to cross open spaces). If you are setting up a bluebird trail, keep the houses at least 100 yd. (91m) from each other.

FINISHING: Although the project can be left unpainted, a coat of exterior primer followed by a top coat of house paint will make the house last longer. Do not paint the inside the house.

You can find hanger strap at most hardware stores.

Use hanger strap and screws to attach your birdhouse to a steel fence post.

Bill of Materials

Qty.	Part	Size of Material
1	Floor	¾" x 3⅛" x 3½" (19 x 79 x 89mm)
1	Ceiling	¾" x 3½" x 5¼" (19 x 79 x 133mm)
1	Front	¾" x 3⁷⁄₁₆" x 7¾" (19 x 87 x 197mm)
2	Side	¾" x 6¾" x 9¼" (19 x 171 x 235mm)
1	Roof	¾" x 9" x 10⅞" (19 x 229 x 276mm)
1	Gusset	1½" x 1½" x 3½" (38 x 38 x 89mm)
1	Tray	1½" x 3½" x 3½" (38 x 89 x 89mm)
1	Back	1½" x 3½" x 14" (38 x 89 x 356mm)
3	Nail	2¼" (57mm)
1	Steel Fence Post	8' (2438mm)

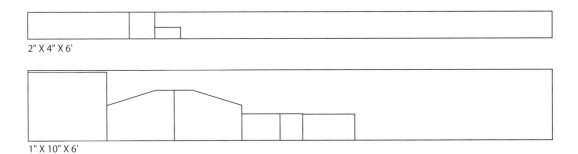

2" X 4" X 6'

1" X 10" X 6'

CUTTING DIAGRAM

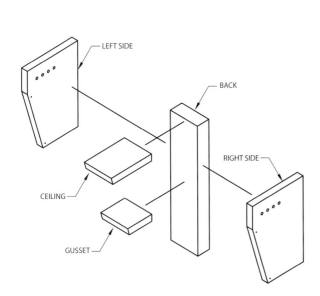

LEFT SIDE

BACK

CEILING

RIGHT SIDE

GUSSET

STEP #1

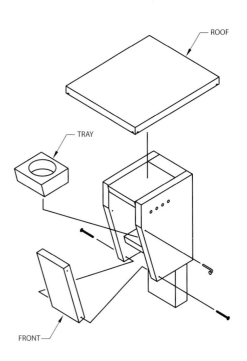

ROOF

TRAY

FRONT

STEP #2

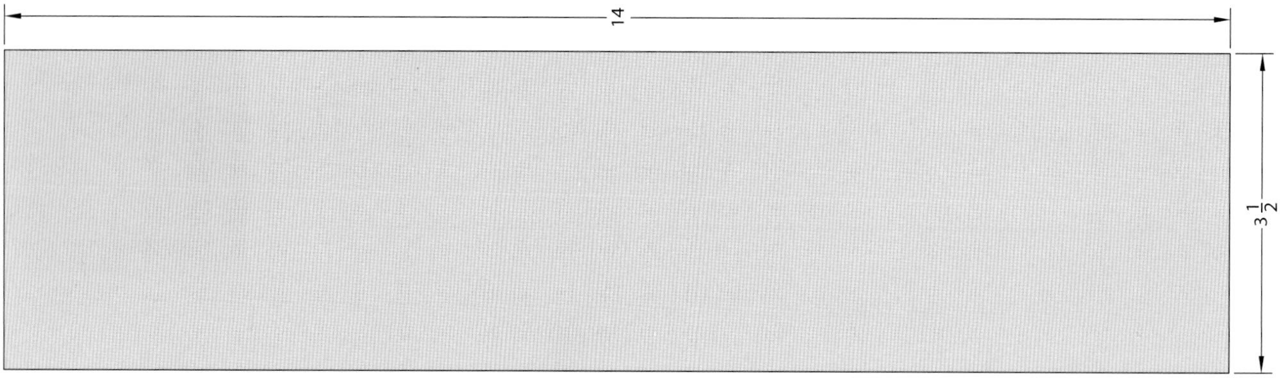

14

BACK
1-1/2" X 3-1/2" X 14"

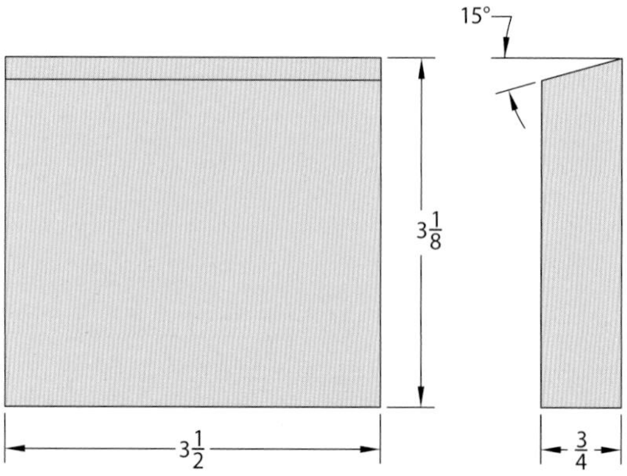

15°

$3\frac{1}{8}$

$3\frac{1}{2}$

$\frac{3}{4}$

FLOOR
3/4" X 3-1/8" X 3-1/2"

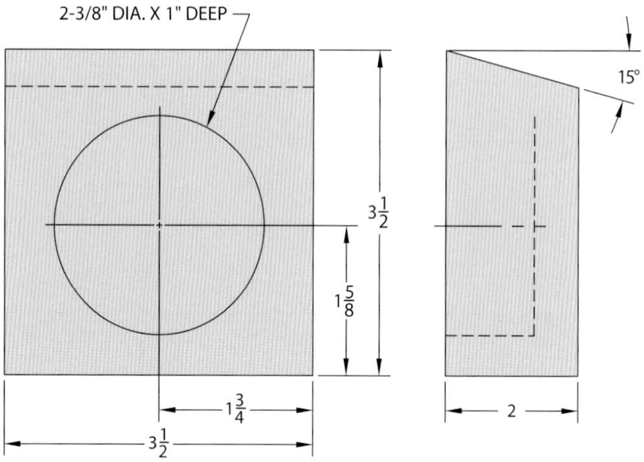

2-3/8" DIA. X 1" DEEP

$3\frac{1}{2}$

$1\frac{5}{8}$

$1\frac{3}{4}$

$3\frac{1}{2}$

15°

2

TRAY
1-1/2" X 3-1/2" X 3-1/2"

15°

$7\frac{3}{4}$

$3\frac{7}{16}$

$\frac{3}{4}$

FRONT
3/4" X 3-7/16" X 7-3/4"

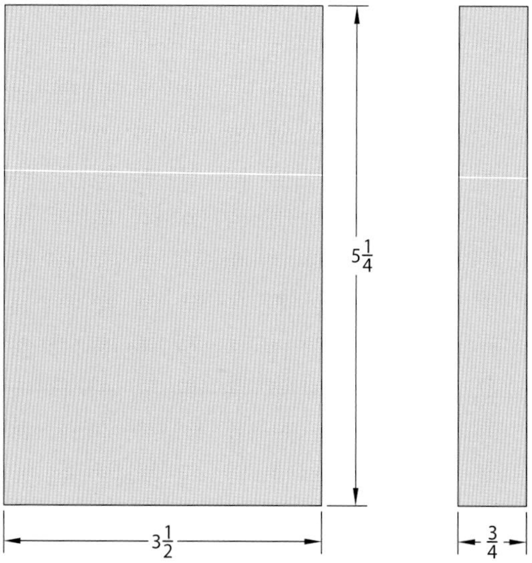

$5\frac{1}{4}$

$3\frac{1}{2}$

$\frac{3}{4}$

CEILING
3/4" X 3-1/2" X 5-1/4"

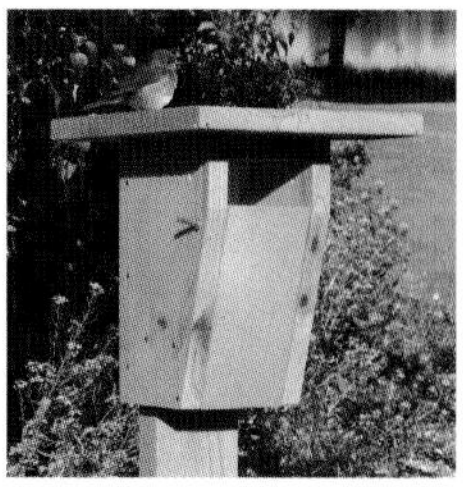

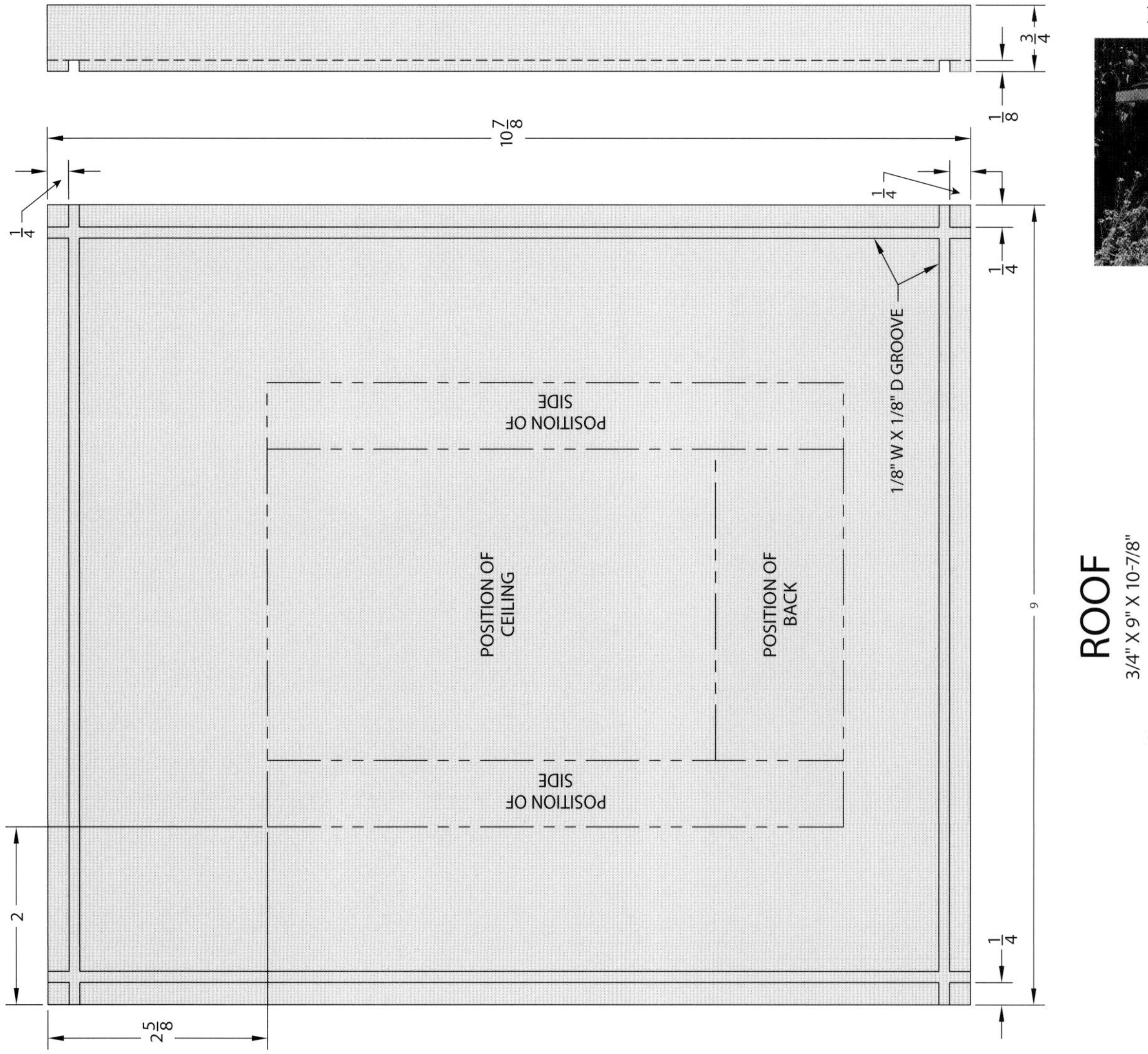
ROOF
3/4" X 9" X 10-7/8"
1/8" W X 1/8" D GROOVE
POSITION OF SIDE
POSITION OF CEILING
POSITION OF BACK
POSITION OF SIDE

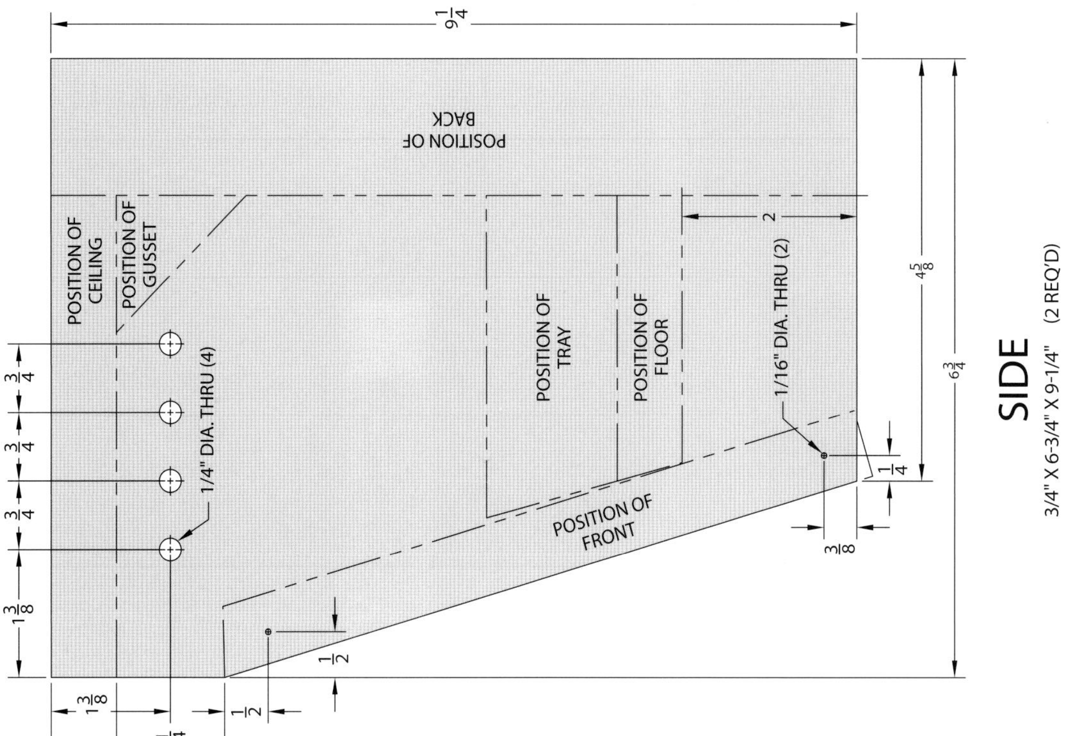
SIDE
3/4" X 6-3/4" X 9-1/4" (2 REQ'D)
POSITION OF BACK
POSITION OF CEILING
POSITION OF GUSSET
POSITION OF TRAY
POSITION OF FLOOR
POSITION OF FRONT
1/4" DIA. THRU (4)
1/16" DIA. THRU (2)

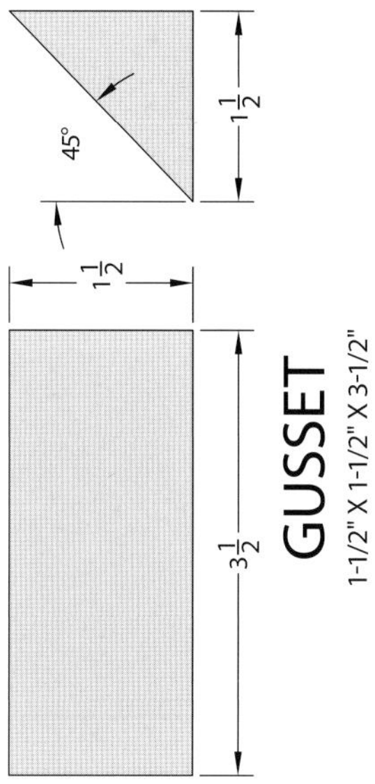
GUSSET
1-1/2" X 1-1/2" X 3-1/2"
45°

Wood Duck House

Wood ducks are among the most beautiful birds in the world. Once plentiful, wood ducks were hunted to precariously low levels by the early 1900s. Today, thanks primarily to protective laws and management, their numbers have increased and stabilized. These population gains have been aided substantially by thousands of man-made nesting boxes.

This wood duck nesting box design has several important features. It opens from the side rather than the top, making it easier to clean. A bent nail holds the door shut. The hole for this nail is drilled down at an angle so it is less likely to fall out. A recess cut into the side of the box below the bottom of the door makes it easy to open. A wood cleat is fastened to the back of the box to tilt the top of the box forward. This slight tilt makes it easier for the ducklings to climb out of the nest box when they are ready to fledge. A hardware cloth screen is securely stapled to the inside of the box below the entrance hole. The hardware cloth provides a footing for the chicks when they are ready to leave the nest box.

Wood duck houses should be inspected at least annually, but the hobby is made much more interesting if the boxes are checked periodically throughout the nesting season. Even if the hens are occasionally flushed from the box during monitoring, abandonment is extremely rare from such an event. She'll come back, and you'll learn a lot. For example, you may find that the box is used twice during the season. A thorough annual inspection should be made in the off-season. Clean the house, check for damage, and make any needed repairs. Be sure to remove and replace the old wood shavings.

In northern climates, wood ducks return to nest shortly after the ice melts in the wetlands. Ideally the box should be ready for them before their return, but otherwise as soon as possible.

A male wood duck.

How-To Instructions

This nest box is made from 1" x 10" (25 x 254mm) and 1" x 12" (25 x 305mm) cedar boards. The Cutting Diagram shows how much lumber you need. The thickness of the cedar boards is called out at ¾" (19mm). However, the project pictured at left was built from ⅞" (22mm) cedar with the rough side facing out. Some minor adjustments were made to the size of the bottom piece to incorporate the ⅞" (22mm) stock.

General assembly of the basic box is done with nails or screws. The advantage of using screws is that you can disassemble the project at a later date if a part needs to be replaced. Two-inch (610mm)-long screws are adequate. Hinge the swinging side door of the house on two screws (nails could be substituted). Be sure to drill appropriate-sized holes for these fasteners. Hold the swinging door closed with a simple latch, which can be made with a 3" (76mm) or slightly larger nail. Drill a

⅛" (3mm) hole in the right side of the Front piece for this latch. Drill it at a downward angle to help keep the nail from falling out. Bend the nail about 1" (25mm) from the head. To open the Side, simply pull out the nail and swing the Side up. For this project, the terms "right" and "left" refer to the right or left side of the project as you face it from the front.

The drawing of the Right Side Bottom piece shows a finger pull—a recess for your finger. Make this by holding the stock against a ¾" (19mm)-diameter drum sander or spindle sander. If a sander isn't available, a round rasp or coarse round file also works for making this finger pull recess.

Begin by cutting each of the parts as described below. Then assemble the project according to the Final Assembly instructions and as shown in the Assembly Drawing.

Keep your ducks safe by using a bent nail to keep the side door closed.

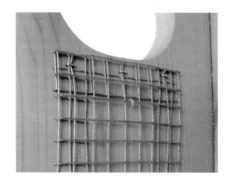

The addition of hardware cloth to the inside of the front of the box makes it easier for chicks to climb up and out.

Use a cleat at the back of the birdhouse to make sure it tilts forward once mounted.

This duckling has just taken its first flight.

TOP AND LEFT SIDE: Lay out and cut to size from ¾" (19mm) stock.

BOTTOM: Lay out and cut to size from ¾" (19mm) stock according to the dimensions given in the Bill of Materials.

RIGHT SIDE: Lay out and cut to size from ¾" (19mm) stock. Drill the ⁷⁄₆₄" (2.8mm)-diameter pilot holes 1¾" (44mm) deep on center. Cut the 45-degree bevel.

RIGHT SIDE BOTTOM: Lay out and cut to size from ¾" (19mm) stock. Cut the 45-degree bevel. Sand the finger pull on a spindle sander or cut with a round rasp or file.

FRONT: Lay out and cut to size from ¾" (19mm) stock. Cut the 10-degree bevel. Drill the ⁹⁄₆₄" (3.6mm)-diameter hole through and countersink for screw. Drill the ⅛" (3mm)-diameter hole through. Cut out the entrance hole.

BACK: Lay out and cut to size from ¾" (19mm) stock. Cut the 10-degree bevel. Drill the ⁹⁄₆₄" (3.6mm)-diameter hole through and countersink for screws where shown.

CLEAT: Lay out and cut to size from ¾" (19mm) stock according to the dimensions given in the Bill of Materials.

HARDWARE CLOTH: Cut to size from ¼" (6mm) hardware cloth. Fold all edges over ½" (13mm) to keep the screen from laying flat against the inside of the Front piece.

SANDING: Finish-sand all parts.

FINAL ASSEMBLY

Staple a piece of hardware cloth to the inside of the Front piece to assist the young ducks when it's time for them to climb out of the box. **IMPORTANT:** This hardware cloth must be securely attached. The hen exits the house multiple times, clawing the screen when she pauses and holds her position at the entrance hole to check her surroundings before exiting the box for incubation breaks. If the top of the hardware cloth pulls away and bends down, it traps the ducklings inside. This also makes it difficult for the hen to enter and leave. An alternative to hardware cloth is to use a table saw to add horizontal saw cuts or to use a router to add "ladder steps" in the wood.

Assemble the box using nails or screws to attach the Front, Back, Bottom, Left Side, and Right Side Bottom pieces together. Attach the Cleat piece to the Back with wood screws. Attach the Top piece to the box assembly.

Although the drawing of the Right Side piece shows it as 8" (203mm) wide, it is best to trim it to 7⅞" (200mm) to allow enough clearance to swing open after rain causes the wood to swell. Attach the Right Side piece with two 2½" (64mm) screws, which will act as hinges (nails could be substituted).

Using the ⅛" (3mm) hole in the Front piece as your drilling guide, extend the hole's depth by drilling further into the Right Side piece to accommodate the 3" (76mm) nail "latch."

FINISHING: We chose not to apply finish to the cedar.

MOUNTING THE BOX: While some people advise mounting the nest box high in a tree, this practice makes it difficult to clean the box and actually puts the ducks in danger from squirrels, minks, and raccoons. Squirrels have been known to take over such boxes and build their own nests in them. Minks and raccoons are known to eat the eggs, nestlings, and even the hen (if they can catch her).

The Wood Duck Society has endorsed a *Best Practices* method that eliminates these problems. They recommend using an 8' (2438mm) steel post like those used for highway stop signs. Steel highway signposts can often be obtained at no charge from the discard pile at a local highway department. These posts can

A finger recess in the Right Side Bottom piece makes it easier to lift the side door.

be used in wet areas or over water as well as on dry ground. Holes are already in place for attaching the box and predator guard. You can use ⁵⁄₁₆" (8mm)-diameter carriage bolts to attach the box to the steel post. Carriage bolts make it easy to remove the box and remount it in a new location or after you have made repairs. Another method is to use a treated landscape timber, flat on two sides, for the post.

If locating the duck house on land, a good location is near a wooded area and close to a wetland, especially one with a strong aquatic insect population. When choosing a location, keep in mind that squirrels have demonstrated they can leap up to 8' (2438mm) horizontally from a tree trunk and drop up to 11' (3353mm) from an overhanging branch. So mount your box a good distance from nearby trees.

Steel posts can be pounded into the ground with a pipe driver or a standard maul (sledge hammer). If using a wood post, use a post-hole digger to make a 2' (610mm)-deep hole for the post. Position the post in the hole so one of the flat sides (the side where the nest box is to be attached) faces toward the flight lane or toward an adjacent wetland. Fill around the post with gravel and tamp the soil firmly to stabilize the post. Mount the box so the entrance hole is 6' (1829mm) from the ground. Attach a metal cone predator guard below the nest box. Dangling polyvinyl chloride (PVC) pipe guards can also be used, but squirrels can sometimes scramble up a PVC pipe after it loses its initial sheen.

Poles can also be mounted in shallow water, but may subject your nest box to dangers from humans, changing water levels or, in freezing temperatures, damage to the pole from shifting ice. Boxes placed on posts in water should be at least 3' (914mm) above the high-water mark.

Bill of Materials

Qty.	Part	Size of Material
1	Top	¾" x 11" x 13" (19 x 279 x 330mm)
1	Bottom	¾" x 7½" x 8" (19 x 191 x 203mm) (not drawn)
1	Left Side	¾" x 8" x 25⅜" (19 x 203 x 645mm)
1	Right Side	¾" x 8" x 19⅛" (19 x 203 x 486mm)
1	Right Side Bottom	¾" x 7" x 8" (19 x 178 x 203mm)
1	Front	¾" x 9" x 24¼" (19 x 229 x 616mm)
1	Back	¾" x 9" x 28¹³⁄₁₆" (19 x 229 x 732mm)
1	Cleat	¾" x 1" x 9" (19 x 25 x 229mm) (not drawn)
1	Lag Screw	5" (127mm) long; ¼" (6mm) diameter
1	Hardware Cloth	¼" x 5" x 13" (6 x 127 x 330mm)
5	#6 Screw	1¼" (32mm)
5	#9 Screw	2½" (64mm)

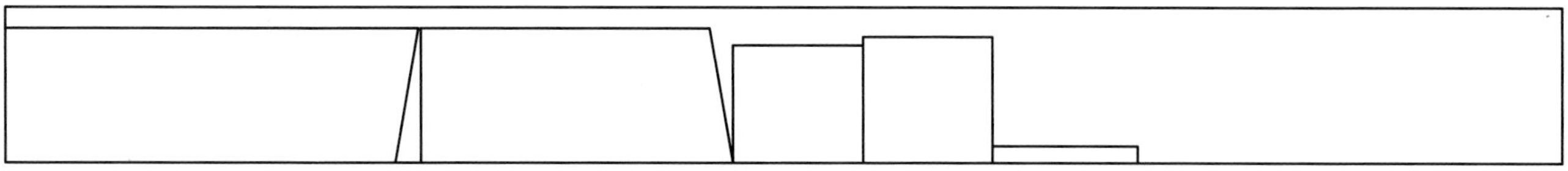

1" X 10" X 8' CEDAR

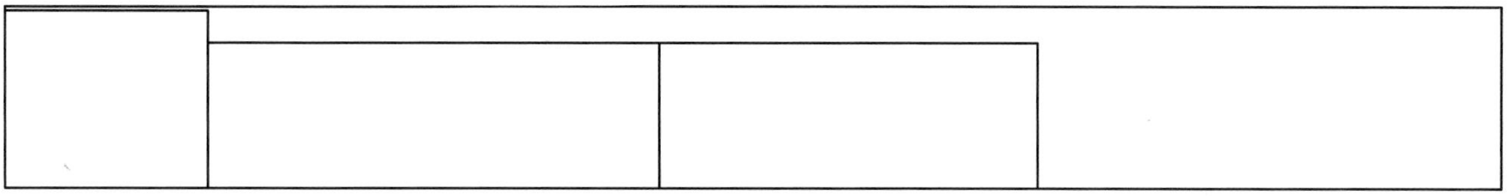

1" X 12" X 8' CEDAR

CUTTING DIAGRAM

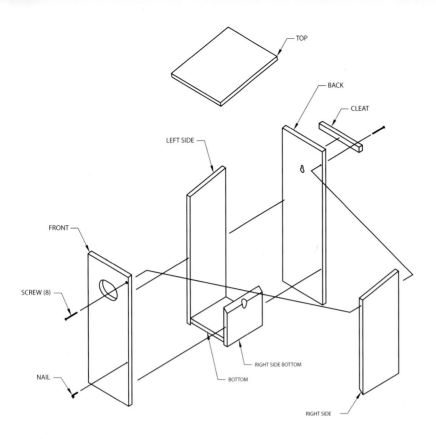

TOP

BACK

CLEAT

LEFT SIDE

FRONT

SCREW (8)

RIGHT SIDE BOTTOM

BOTTOM

NAIL

RIGHT SIDE

ASSEMBLY DRAWING

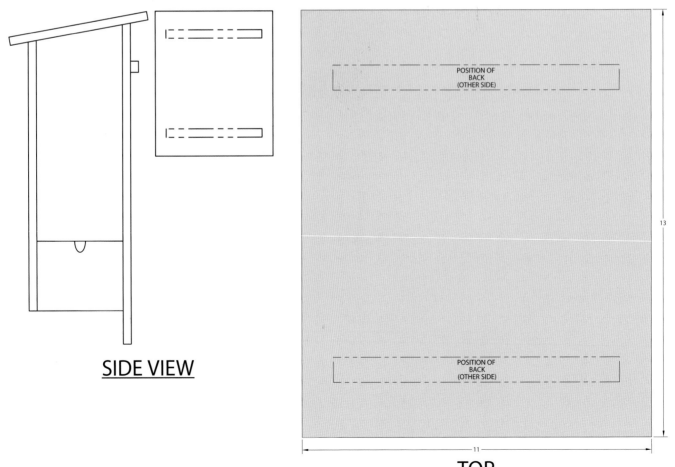

SIDE VIEW

POSITION OF
BACK
(OTHER SIDE)

POSITION OF
BACK
(OTHER SIDE)

13

11

TOP
3/4" X 11" X 13"

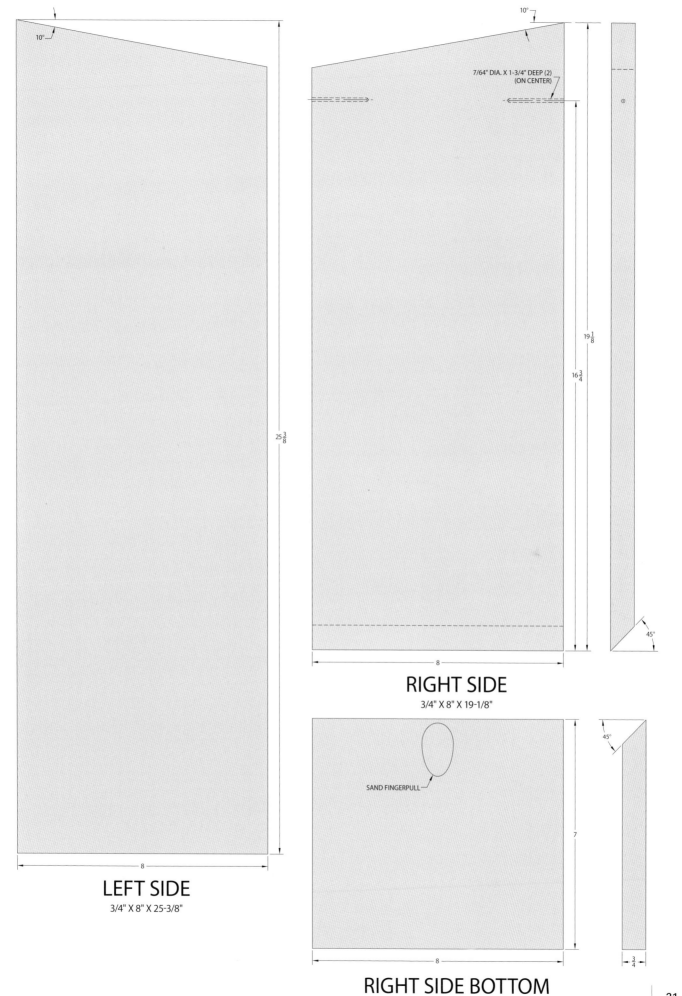

10°

10°

7/64" DIA. X 1-3/4" DEEP (2)
(ON CENTER)

$19\frac{1}{8}$

$16\frac{3}{4}$

45°

8

RIGHT SIDE
3/4" X 8" X 19-1/8"

$25\frac{3}{8}$

8

LEFT SIDE
3/4" X 8" X 25-3/8"

45°

SAND FINGERPULL

7

8

$\frac{3}{4}$

RIGHT SIDE BOTTOM
3/4" X 7" X 8"

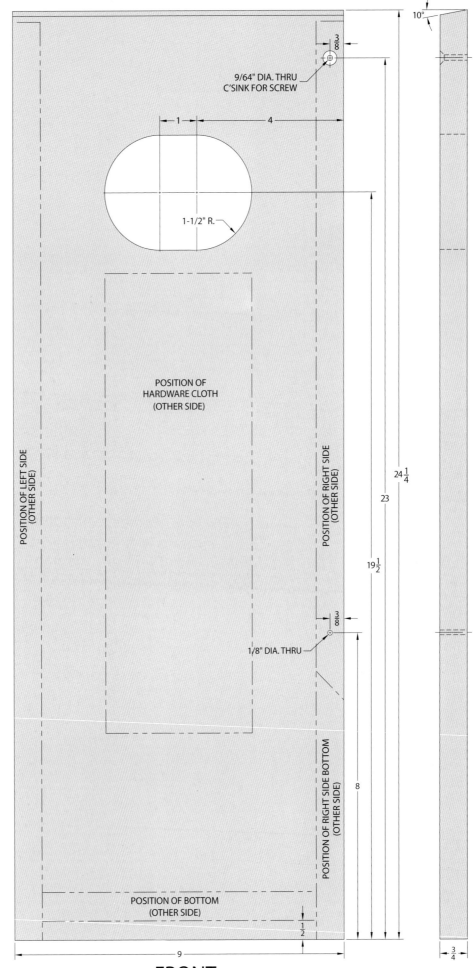

10°

3/8

9/64" DIA. THRU
C'SINK FOR SCREW

1   4

1-1/2" R.

POSITION OF
HARDWARE CLOTH
(OTHER SIDE)

POSITION OF LEFT SIDE
(OTHER SIDE)

POSITION OF RIGHT SIDE
(OTHER SIDE)

24 1/4

23

19 1/2

3/8

1/8" DIA. THRU

POSITION OF RIGHT SIDE BOTTOM
(OTHER SIDE)

8

POSITION OF BOTTOM
(OTHER SIDE)

1/2

9

3/4

FRONT
3/4" X 9" X 24-1/4"

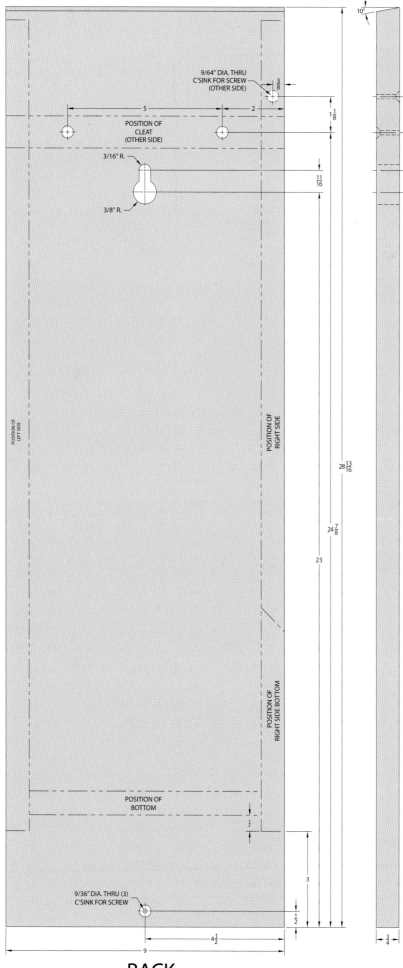

Wood Duck House

10°

9/64" DIA. THRU
C'SINK FOR SCREW
(OTHER SIDE)

3/8

5   2

1 1/8

POSITION OF
CLEAT
(OTHER SIDE)

3/16" R.

11/16

3/8" R.

POSITION OF
LEFT SIDE

POSITION OF
RIGHT SIDE

28 13/16

24 7/8

23

POSITION OF
RIGHT SIDE BOTTOM

POSITION OF
BOTTOM

1/2

3

9/36" DIA. THRU (3)
C'SINK FOR SCREW

1/2

4 1/2

9

3/4

BACK

3/4" X 9" X 28-13/16"

Window View Birdhouse

This birdhouse provides the perfect way to bird-watch. The clear plastic panel in back allows you to observe how the nest is built, monitor the progress as eggs are laid, and see the baby birds hatch. The feeding of the babies is amazing to watch. The small birds impatiently wait for the adult to drop the next morsel of food into their wide-open mouths. You can witness the first awkward attempts at flying when the little ones are ready to fledge. And all this from the comfort of your favorite chair by the window! This project provides an educational experience for you as well as your children or grandchildren.

The cavity size is suitable for chickadees, nuthatches, and titmice. You can increase the entrance hole size to 1½" (38mm) or 1¾" (44mm) to attract larger birds (see Appendix C.)

For versatility, use chain to hang the birdhouse. Locate it under the house eaves, with the back of the birdhouse facing your window.

Did you know? Some people believe the best time to put out a birdhouse is in the fall, thinking it will weather and be ready for a family to take over in the spring. The truth is that you can put your birdhouse out any time of the year. Although birds tend to nest earlier in the warmer southern states than in the cooler northern states, there is no guarantee they will nest at all the first year. Even if your entrance hole and cavity size is correct, your location is acceptable and there is food and water available, it might take two or three years for birds to accept a birdhouse as part of their natural environment. Be patient! The most important thing is that you make the effort to try and help our native American birds.

How-To Instructions

The project pictured was constructed from cedar, but pine or other woods could be substituted. The Cutting Diagram shows how much lumber you'll need. Although ¾" (19mm) lumber is specified in the Bill of Materials and on the plan drawings, cedar boards are sometimes slightly thicker than ¾" (19mm). Stock up to ⅞" (22mm) thick can be used with this design. However, using stock thicker than ¾" (19mm) may require you to make some size adjustments.

The majority of the assembly is done with water-resistant glue and finishing nails. Do not glue the bottom, so you can remove it to clean out old nests. The plan shows screw clearance holes drilled and countersunk in the Side pieces. These holes allow you to attach the Bottom piece with #6 2" (51mm) wood screws.

Cedar is sometimes sold with one smooth side and one rough side. We faced the rough side out on all pieces.

The entrance hole size is called out at 1¼" (32mm). This diameter size can be changed as desired depending on the species of bird you are trying to attract.

Although not shown, remember to drill ⅜" (10mm) air-vent holes along the top of the Side pieces just under the roof edges and ¼" (6mm) drain holes in the Bottom piece.

To hang the project, place two screw eyes along the peak of the roof approximately 1" (25mm) from each end. Attach a length of #16 jack chain (or equivalent) to each screw eye. Using pliers, open the chain link just far enough to slip it onto the screw eye. Squeeze the link to close it. Hang the birdhouse from screw eyes installed under the eaves of your house. Be sure to position the birdhouse in front of a window so it is convenient to watch.

Begin by cutting each of the parts as described below. Then, assemble the project according to the Final Assembly instructions and as shown in the Assembly Drawing.

BOTTOM, BACK, ROOF A, AND ROOF B: Lay out and cut to size from ¾" (19mm) stock.

SIDE: Lay out and cut to size from ¾" (19mm) stock. Cut the 45-degree bevel. Cut the ⅛" x ⅛" (3 x 3mm) groove. Drill the %4" (3.6mm)-diameter holes through and countersink for screws. (One right-hand and one left-hand piece required.)

FRONT: Lay out and cut to size from ¾" (19mm) stock. Drill the 1¼" (32mm)-diameter hole through.

SANDING: Finish-sand all parts.

FINAL ASSEMBLY

STEP 1: Glue and nail the Side pieces to the Front and Back pieces. Slip the acrylic plastic in the ⅛" (3mm) grooves in the Side pieces and attach the removable Bottom piece with screws.

STEP 2: Center the Roof A and Roof B pieces and attach with glue and nails.

FINISHING: The completed birdhouse can be painted or stained. If you are building the project from cedar or redwood, you may choose to omit applying any type of wood finish. Do not apply wood finish to the interior of the box.

HANGING THE PROJECT: Drill ³⁄₃₂" (2.5mm) holes approximately 1" to 1½" (25 to 38mm) from each end of the roof peak and install the screw eyes. Attach a length of #16 jack chain (or equivalent) to each screw eye. Using pliers, open the chain link just far enough to slip it onto the screw eye.

Bill of Materials

Qty.	Part	Size of Material
1	Bottom	¾" x 4¾" x 5¾" (19 x 121 x 146mm)
1	Roof A	¾" x 5¼" x 8" (19 x 133 x 203mm)
1	Roof B	¾" x 6" x 8" (19 x 152 x 203mm)
2	Side	¾" x 5¾" x 8½" (19 x 146 x 216mm)
1	Back	¾" x 3⅛" x 4¾" (19 x 79 x 121mm)
1	Front	¾" x 6¼" x 10⅞" (19 x 159 x 276mm)
1	Clear Acrylic Plastic	5" x 7" (127x 178mm)
4	#6 Screw	2" (51mm)
4	Screw Eye	1⁹⁄₁₆" (40mm)
1	#16 Chain	12' (3658mm)

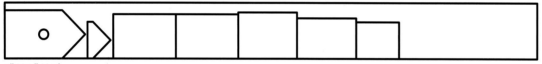

1" X 8" X 6'

CUTTING DIAGRAM

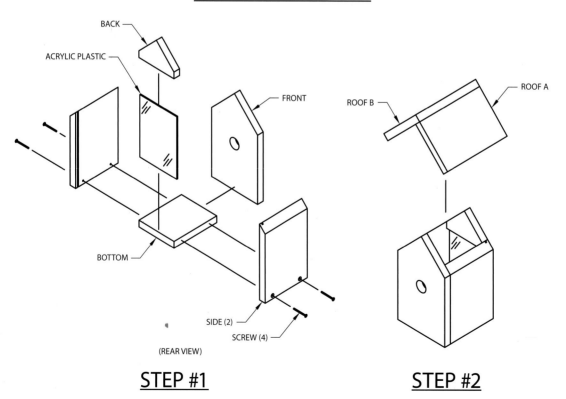

BACK

ACRYLIC PLASTIC

FRONT

BOTTOM

SIDE (2)

SCREW (4)

(REAR VIEW)

STEP #1

ROOF B

ROOF A

STEP #2

ROOF A
3/4" X 5-1/4" X 8"

$5\frac{1}{4}$

8

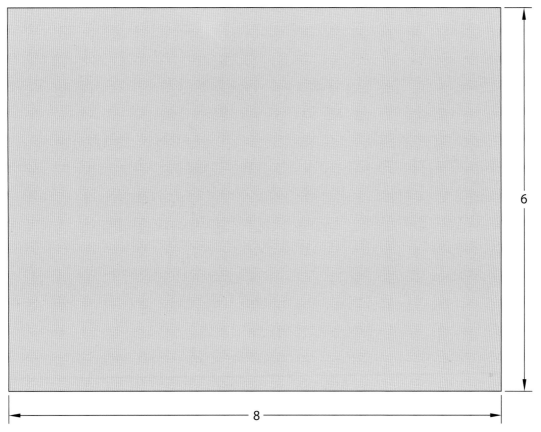

ROOF B
3/4" X 6" X 8"

6

8

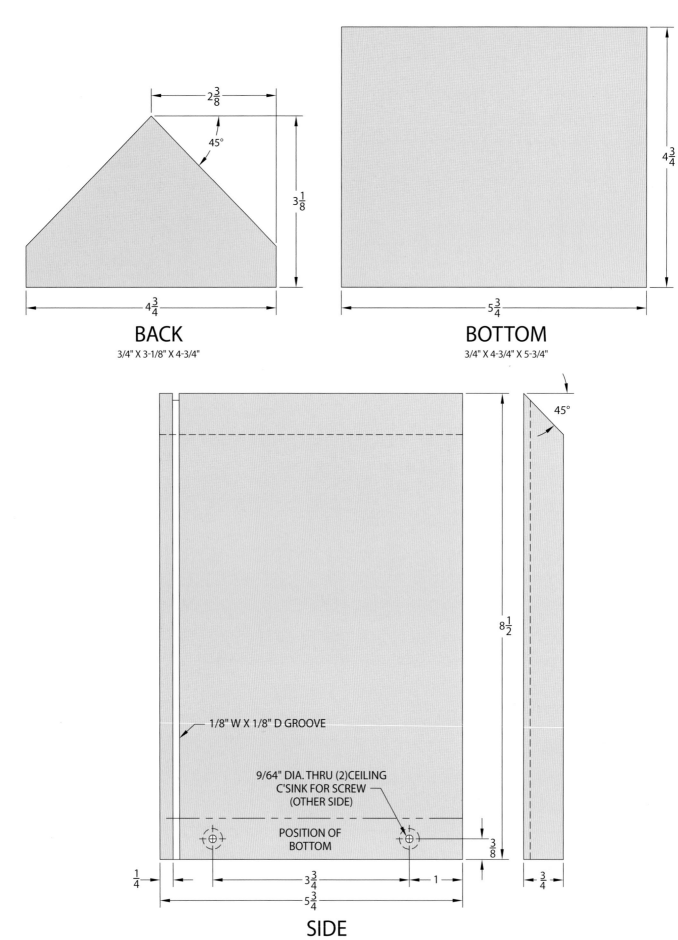

BACK
3/4" X 3-1/8" X 4-3/4"

BOTTOM
3/4" X 4-3/4" X 5-3/4"

$2\frac{3}{8}$

45°

$3\frac{1}{8}$

$4\frac{3}{4}$

$4\frac{3}{4}$

$5\frac{3}{4}$

45°

1/8" W X 1/8" D GROOVE

$8\frac{1}{2}$

9/64" DIA. THRU (2) CEILING
C'SINK FOR SCREW
(OTHER SIDE)

POSITION OF
BOTTOM

$\frac{3}{8}$

$\frac{1}{4}$

$3\frac{3}{4}$

1

$5\frac{3}{4}$

$\frac{3}{4}$

SIDE
3/4" X 5-3/4" X 8-1/2"   (1 RH & 1 LH REQ'D)   (RH SHOWN)

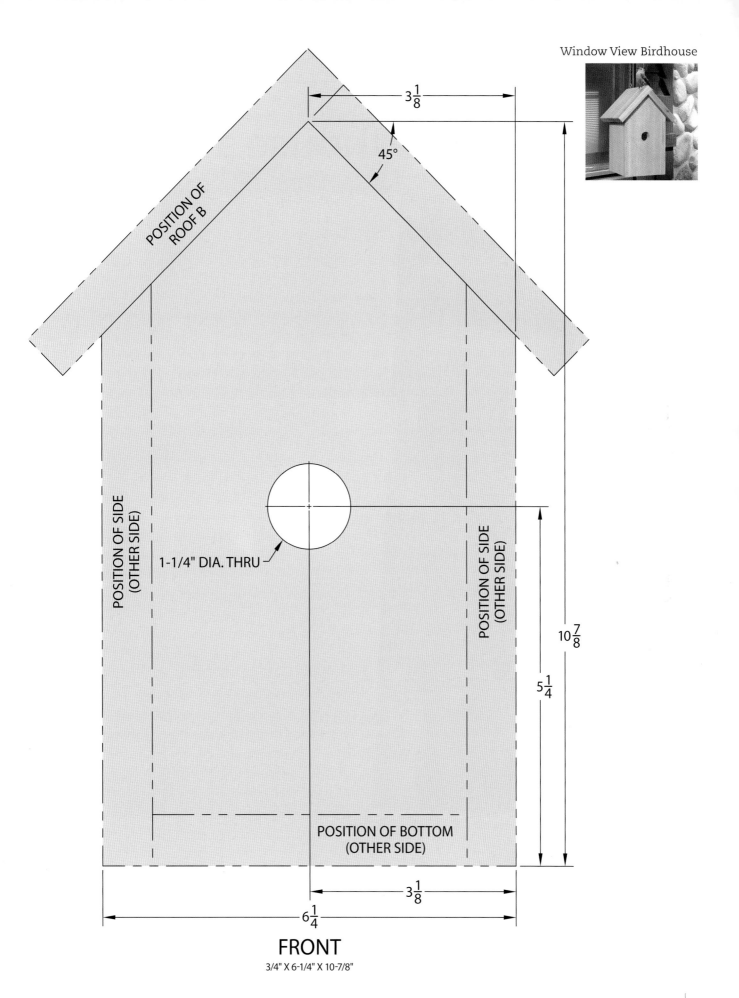

Window View Birdhouse

$3\frac{1}{8}$

45°

POSITION OF
ROOF B

POSITION OF SIDE
(OTHER SIDE)

POSITION OF SIDE
(OTHER SIDE)

1-1/4" DIA. THRU

$10\frac{7}{8}$

$5\frac{1}{4}$

POSITION OF BOTTOM
(OTHER SIDE)

$3\frac{1}{8}$

$6\frac{1}{4}$

FRONT

3/4" X 6-1/4" X 10-7/8"

Chickadee Birdhouse and Roost

Clean your birdhouse by swinging open the front panel.

This project serves two purposes: The top is a nesting cavity for chickadees to build their nests, while the bottom section serves as a "warmer." Chickadees are non-migratory, meaning they stay throughout the winter, toughing out the cold northern climate. One way they keep warm is by huddling together in a place sheltered from the wind. The lower portion of this birdhouse provides such a place and is called a roost box—a place where several pairs of chickadees can gather together to stay warm. Because heat rises, the entrance hole for the roost section is located near the bottom. Several wood dowel perches are located on the inside. The project is designed so the entire front swings open for cleaning.

The black-capped chickadee is easy to identify with its distinctive black marking on the top of the head, black bib (the area under his beak), gray-black wings and tail, and whitish underside. Their large round heads and small bodies give them a cute appearance. Chickadees are naturally curious birds that investigate everything in their immediate habitat—including humans. They are even known to accept food from a person's hand once they become comfortable with their surroundings. They are quick to adopt a feeder and frequent it regularly, even though their main diet consists of insects and berries. They are pleasant birds to watch as they perform acrobatic-like feats, catching insects on the fly.

These cute and friendly birds are a pleasant addition to your yard. Offering summer and winter housing helps ensure their presence year round. Another benefit that you may notice is a decrease in the amount of insects around your yard!

How-To Instructions

This project is constructed from ¾" (19mm) lumber. It is pictured in pine, although other wood varieties can certainly be used. Most assembly can be done with finishing nails and water-resistant glue. The amount of material you will need is shown in the Cutting Diagram.

Hinge the Door at the top on two 2¼" (57mm) nails. Latch the Door with a loose pin: another 2¼" (57mm) nail bent over as shown on step 2 of the Assembly Drawing. These pins can be placed on one or both sides. By pulling the lower pin(s), you can open the Door to examine or clean the inside cavities. The holes are called out in the drawing of the Side piece as being 1/16" (4mm) in diameter. This size should be adjusted depending on the diameter of the nails you are using. Drill the hole for the loose pin(s) as close as possible to the diameter of the nail, but no smaller. The loose pins should be easy to remove.

Drill two ¼" (6mm) mounting holes in the Back piece so the project can be secured to a vertical surface. Mount it from 5' to 15' (1524 to 4572mm) above ground. Face it toward the south for protection against winter winds.

Begin by cutting each of the parts as described below. Then, assemble the project according to the Final Assembly instructions and as shown in the Assembly Drawing.

The curious chickadee has distinctive black coloring.

Dangerous Wood

Do not build birdhouses or bird feeders with lumber that has been treated under pressure with green preservative (chromated copper arsenate). This wood, usually pine or a similarly light-colored wood, is deemed acceptable for human contact (such as when used to make a picnic table), but is not necessarily safe for birds. Two acceptable woods to use are cedar and pine. Cedar is especially recommended for projects with a natural finish (or no finish at all). For projects that will be painted, pine is satisfactory and less expensive than cedar. Never stain or paint the *inside* of your bird feeders or birdhouses.

TIP: Without air vents, birdhouses can turn into bird ovens. Two common ways to add ventilation are to leave gaps between the roof and sides of the box or to drill ⅜" to ½" (10 to 13mm)-diameter holes in both sides of the birdhouse, just below the roof. Both methods provide fresh air and help disperse heat.

FLOOR: Lay out and cut to size from ¾" (19mm) stock. Drill the ¼" (6mm)-diameter drain hole through. (Two pieces required.)

DOOR: Lay out and cut to size from ¾" (19mm) stock. Cut the 15-degree bevel. Drill the 1⅛" (3mm)-diameter holes through.

BACK: Lay out and cut to size from ¾" (19mm) stock. Drill the ¼" (6mm)-diameter mounting holes through.

SIDE: Lay out and cut to size from ¾" (19mm) stock. Mark, but do not drill, the 1/16" (2mm)-diameter holes at this time. Drill the ¼" (6mm)-diameter holes ¼" (6mm) deep for the dowels on the inside face of each piece. Drill the ¼" (6mm)-diameter holes through for ventilation. (One right-hand and one left-hand piece required.)

ROOF: Lay out and cut to size from ¾" (19mm) stock. Cut the 15-degree bevel.

DOWEL: Lay out and cut to length from ¼" (6mm) dowel stock according to the Bill of Materials. (Three pieces required.)

SANDING: Finish-sand all parts.

FINAL ASSEMBLY

STEP 1: Glue and nail the Back piece to one of the Side pieces in the position shown on the drawing of the Back piece. Attach the two Floor pieces to the Back and Side. Position the three dowels (with glue on each of the ends) and attach the remaining Side piece. The dowels should not rotate in the finished assembly.

STEP 2: Attach the Roof to the Sides and Back. Place the Door between the Side pieces in the position shown on the drawing of the Side piece. The top of the Door piece should be ⅛" (3mm) from the bottom of the Roof piece. With the Door in position, pre-drill the upper holes through the Sides and into the Door with a drill bit just slightly smaller than the nail being used. With the Door still in position, drill the bottom holes through the Side pieces and into the Door with a drill bit as close as possible to the diameter of the nail being used.

Remove the Door and re-drill the top holes in the Side pieces with a drill bit slightly larger than the nails. Drive two nails through the top holes in the Side piece and into the Door piece to act as hinges. Insert bent nail(s) in the bottom to act as a latch(es).

FINISHING: Stain or paint as desired. Do not finish the interior of the project.

Bill of Materials

Qty.	Part	Size of Material
2	Floor	¾" x 4½" x 6½" (19 x 114 x 165mm)
1	Door	¾" x 4½" x 20⅜" (19 x 114 x 518mm)
1	Back	¾" x 6" x 26" (19 x 152 x 660mm)
2	Side	¾" x 7¼" x 22¼" (19 x 184 x 565mm)
1	Roof	¾" x 7¼" x 9" (19 x 184 x 229mm)
3	Dowel	¼" (6mm) diameter; 5" (127mm) long
4	Nail	2¼" (57mm)

Note: An aluminum pop rivet can be substituted for the latch nail.

TIP: Birds sometimes fly into your window because they see the reflection of the sky or the woods. The more birds you attract to your yard, the greater the likelihood of window collisions. Black window decals in the shape of flying birds have been suggested as a solution, but have not been proven to prevent these collisions. Thin netting hung outside a large window does help, however.

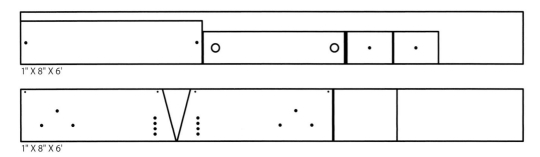

1" X 8" X 6'

1" X 8" X 6'

CUTTING DIAGRAM

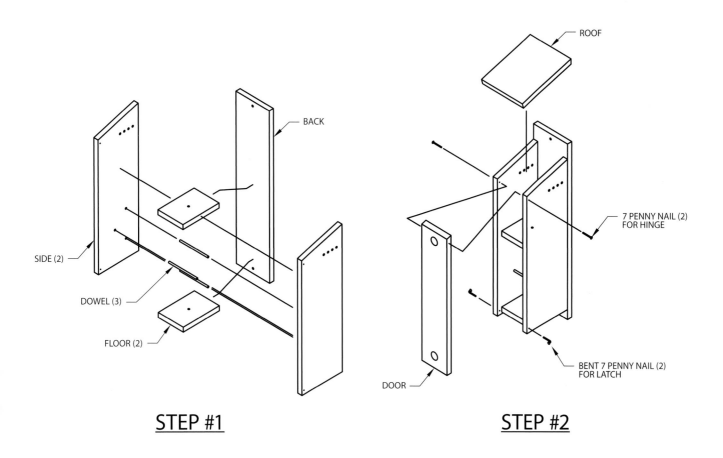

ROOF

BACK

SIDE (2)

DOWEL (3)

FLOOR (2)

7 PENNY NAIL (2)
FOR HINGE

DOOR

BENT 7 PENNY NAIL (2)
FOR LATCH

STEP #1

STEP #2

15°

9

7 1/4

3/4

ROOF
3/4" X 7-1/4" X 9"

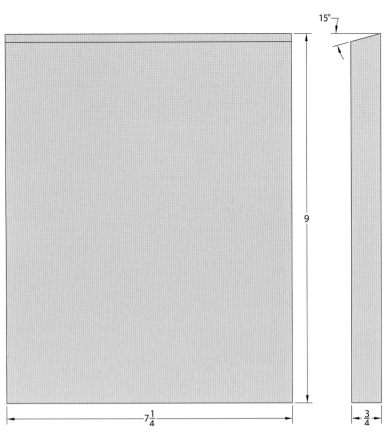

1/4" DIA. THRU

4 1/2

2 1/4

3 1/4

6 1/2

FLOOR
3/4" X 4-1/2" X 6-1/2"   (2 REQ'D)

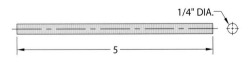

1/4" DIA.

5

DOWEL
3/4" X 4-1/2" X 20-3/8"   (3 REQ'D)

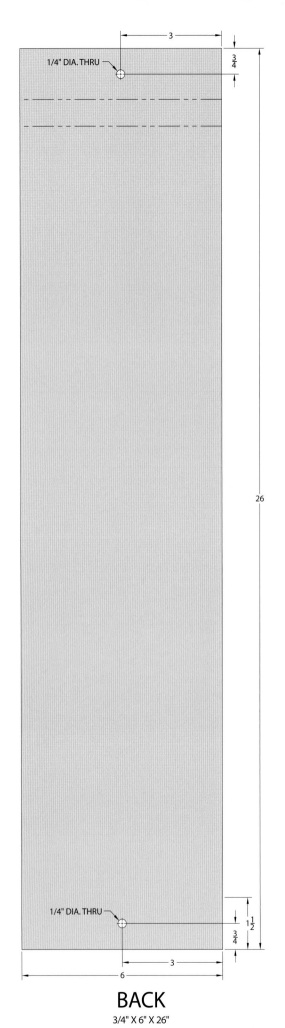

3

3/4

1/4" DIA. THRU

26

1/4" DIA. THRU

1 1/2

3/4

3

6

BACK
3/4" X 6" X 26"

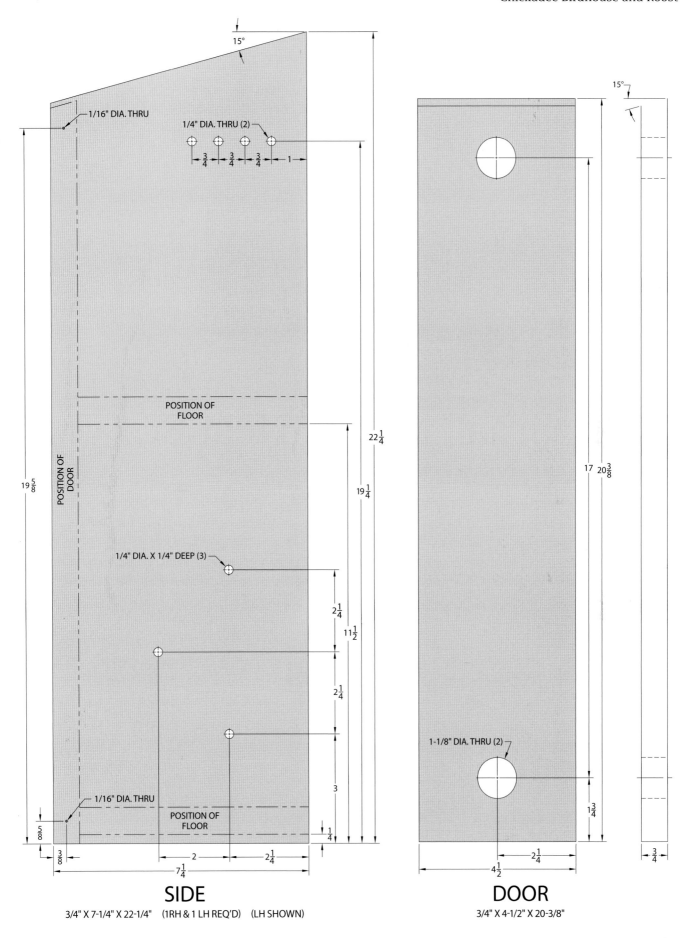

SIDE
3/4" X 7-1/4" X 22-1/4" (1RH & 1 LH REQ'D) (LH SHOWN)

DOOR
3/4" X 4-1/2" X 20-3/8"

Small Raptor Nest Box

This house is designed for small raptors, including the American kestrel, the northern screech owl, and the northern saw-whet owl. These three species are small: the American kestrel is about the size of an American robin; northern screech owl about 8" (203mm) high; and the northern saw-whet owl—one of the smallest United States owls—only about 7" (178mm) high.

Due to their small size, the diet of these raptors is limited to small prey, such as large insects, and a wide range of rodents, including mice, rats, shrews, and moles. Be cautioned: these raptors are all predators. They can also take small birds, so this box should not be placed in an urban backyard. A better location is in a hardwood forest, preferably on the edge of the woods adjacent to a field or a wetland.

Because of the 3" (76mm)-diameter entrance hole, sparrows, starlings, and even squirrels may move into this nesting cavity. Because sparrows and starlings are not protected, you can remove and destroy their eggs, making the house again available to a raptor. Preventing squirrels from taking over the box is more difficult. In some cases a sheet metal band around the tree trunk may prevent squirrels from climbing the tree, but this is only effective where squirrels cannot gain access by jumping from an adjoining tree. The best solution is to keep squirrels out in the first place. Do this by mounting the nest box on a steel post (or on a wood post with a predator guard). The house should be mounted at least 10' (3048mm) above ground.

TIP: Wood ducks, American kestrels, screech owls, and northern saw-whet owls prefer wood shavings placed in the bottom of their nest boxes. Wood shavings can usually be found at no charge from cabinet shops or sawmills. Wood chips and shavings are much preferred over sawdust, which is much finer and tends to collect and hold moisture.

INTERESTING FACTS ABOUT THE AMERICAN KESTREL

The American kestrel is perhaps the most colorful raptor in the world. It is also the most common falcon in North America. It can be found in Alaska, most of Canada, and in each of the continental states. Although United States law governs the use of raptors by falconers, apprentice falconers sometimes train the American kestrel to hunt non-game species, such as insects, sparrows, and starlings.

When nesting, kestrel nestlings back up, raise their tails and squirt feces and urine out of the nest and directly onto the cavity walls, where the excrement dries. This keeps the baby chicks and the nest clean, but causes the inside of the nesting box to smell awful!

The state of Iowa implemented a program to place kestrel nest boxes on the back of information signs along Interstate Highway 35. The grassy interstate right-of-way is an ideal habitat for kestrels, and the metal signposts prevent predators such as cats and raccoons from reaching the nest boxes. It has been reported approximately 40–60 percent of these boxes are inhabited by kestrels.

INTERESTING FACTS ABOUT SCREECH OWLS AND SAW-WHET OWLS

Northern screech owls are small gray or reddish owls that resemble a miniature version of the great horned owl. They prefer nest boxes at least 10' (3048mm) off the ground and on the edges of a hardwood forests adjacent to fields or wetlands.

The northern saw-whet owl is one of our smallest owls. Less common than the screech owl, it is seldom seen. It prefers nest boxes 14' (4267mm) off the ground and placed in live mature trees.

American kestrel.

Northern screech owl.

Northern saw-whet owl.

WORDS TO KNOW

Falcon: Any hawk trained to kill small game. In falconry, the female is called a falcon and the male a tiercel.

Falconer: A person who breeds and trains falcons.

Hawk: Birds with short rounded wings, long tails and legs, and a hooked beak and claws. More broadly, any such bird active by day, except vultures and eagles. Hawks include the falcons and buzzards.

Owl: Any of an order of night birds of prey distinguished by a large flat face, eyes surrounded by stiff-feathered disks, a short hooked beak, feathered legs with sharp talons, and soft plumage permitting noiseless flight. The name is derived from the Latin *ululare*, "to howl."

Raptor: One who seizes by force; a bird of prey such as a hawk, eagle, or owl.

How-To Instructions

This project is constructed from ¾" (19mm) stock that is cut, sanded, and glued together. Joints may be reinforced with nails or screws as desired.

Begin by cutting each of the parts as described below. Then, assemble the project according to the Final Assembly instructions and as shown in the Assembly Drawing.

BOTTOM: Lay out and cut to size from ¾" (19mm) stock. Drill the ¼" (6mm)-diameter drain holes through.

TOP: Lay out and cut to size from ¾" (19mm) stock.

FRONT: Lay out and cut to size from ¾" (19mm) stock. Cut the 3" (17mm)-diameter hole.

SIDE: Lay out and cut to size from ¾" (19mm) stock. Drill the ½" (13mm)-diameter air-vent holes through. (Two pieces required.)

BACK: Lay out and cut to size from ¾" (19mm) stock. Drill the ½" (13mm)-diameter mounting holes through.

SANDING: Finish-sand all parts.

FINAL ASSEMBLY

Attach the Bottom and Side pieces to the Back where shown. Note the Bottom piece is inset ¼" (6mm) to help keep rainwater from leaking into the cavity. Attach the Front to the Bottom and Sides. Attach the Top to the Back where shown with the hinges to allow for later cleaning. Attach the hook and screw eyes to the Top and one or both of the Side pieces. They should be tight enough to prevent predators from opening the nest box.

FINISHING: This project can be left unfinished or it can be painted or stained as desired. Do not apply wood finish to the interior of the box.

TIP: Using nails or screws to hang a birdhouse from a tree is extremely unlikely to kill the tree. Trees heal differently than animals, by a process scientists call CODIT: compartmentalization of decay in trees. When a tree is wounded, microorganisms (mainly fungi) enter and cause decay. The tree responds by isolating the affected area, forming a compartment of which the side walls are rays (lines radiating from the center of the tree) and the back is the first annular growth ring not damaged by the wound. The top and bottom are formed after wounding when the elements that transport liquids become plugged. In most cases, this keeps decay from spreading.

Bill of Materials

Qty.	Part	Size of Material
1	Bottom	¾" x 7¾" x 9¼" (19 x 197 x 235mm)
1	Top	¾" x 9¼" x 12" (19 x 235 x 305mm)
1	Front	¾" x 9¼" x 16" (19 x 235 x 406mm)
2	Side	¾" x 9¼" x 16" (19 x 235 x 406mm)
1	Back	¾" x 9¼" x 22" (19 x 235 x 559mm)
1 pair	Hinge	
2	Hook w/ Screw Eye	

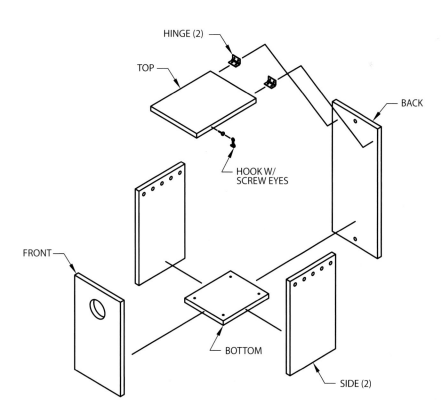

ASSEMBLY DRAWING

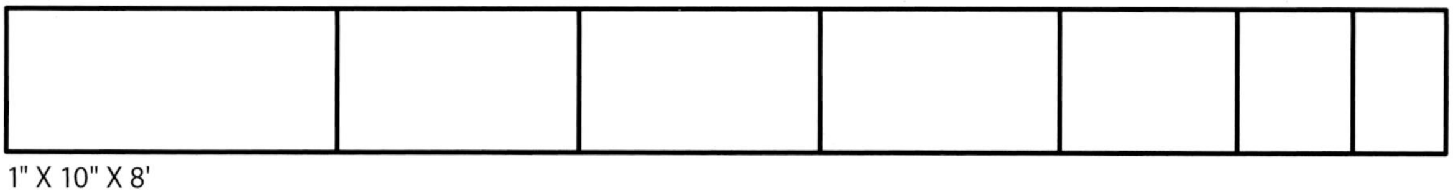

1" X 10" X 8'

CUTTING DIAGRAM

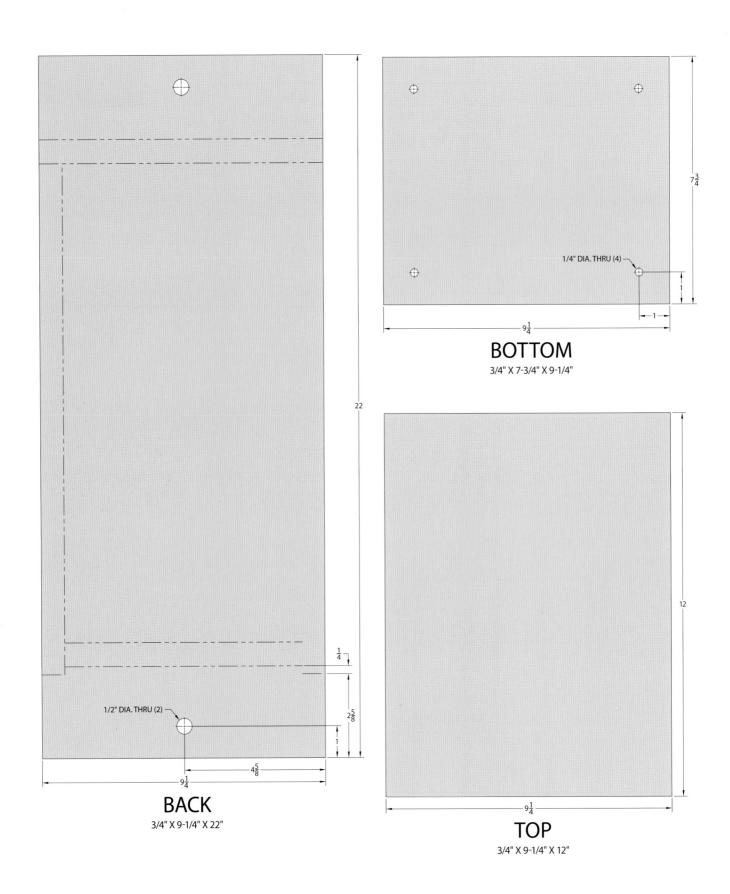

BOTTOM
3/4" X 7-3/4" X 9-1/4"

1/4" DIA. THRU (4)

7¾

9¼

1

1

BACK
3/4" X 9-1/4" X 22"

1/2" DIA. THRU (2)

22

¼

2⅝

1

4⅝

9¼

TOP
3/4" X 9-1/4" X 12"

12

9¼

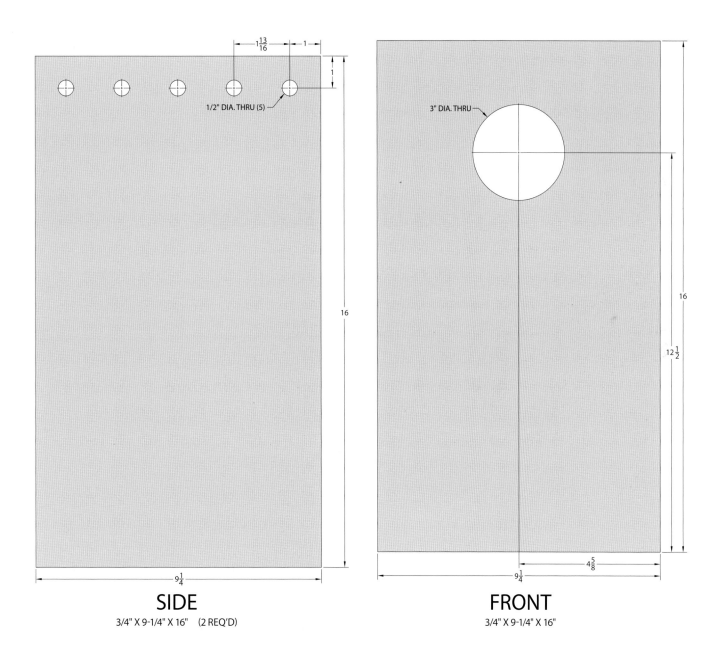

13/16   1

1/2" DIA. THRU (5)

3" DIA. THRU

16

16

12 1/2

9 1/4

9 1/4

4 5/8

SIDE
3/4" X 9-1/4" X 16"   (2 REQ'D)

FRONT
3/4" X 9-1/4" X 16"

Martin House

Purple martins are one of the most desirable and most loved bird species. They provide constant entertainment as they perform breathtaking maneuvers, catching insects as they fly about. Martins like to be around people, and martin enthusiasts, often referred to as *landlords*, are passionate about attracting these wonderful birds and keeping their colony well maintained. You can identify purple martins by their dark purple color and cheerful chirps.

Martins do not have the ability to make their own nesting cavities and so depend on dedicated landlords to provide and maintain housing for them. Martins reward landlords for their efforts with constant singing (or at least pleasant chirps and calls). Maintaining a martin house, called a *colony*, does take some dedication, but once you attract families to your structure, they will return year after year.

Providing a martin house that conforms to the needs of these birds is an essential step to attracting them in the first place. This project offers several important improvements over other martin-house designs. One of the most important features is that the front, back, and balconies are built as one assembly. By rotating four-turn buttons, these assemblies can be removed to inspect the nests or clean the cavities. In addition, the cavity partitions and floors can be taken out, making cleaning exceptionally easy. This house is inexpensive to make and, for a wooden structure, exceptionally light.

The plan also includes the design for a telescopic pole that allows you to lower the house for inspection and cleaning. The house is made so the pole can extend through the center while you lower the house for inspection or maintenance.

TIP: You can assist nest-building birds by providing short pieces of string, yarn, fiber scraps, or even thin ribbon. Cut them into lengths no longer than 4 to 6 inches (102 to 152mm). (Birds can entangle themselves with longer pieces of string.) Drape them over branches separated from each other so the individual strings won't become tangled, and they'll be easy for the birds to pick up.

How-To Instructions

This project uses ¼" (6mm) exterior plywood and ¾" (19mm) pine. The Cutting Diagram shows the amount of material you will need. A small amount of curl or distortion in the plywood will be corrected after you nail and glue the ¼" (6mm) plywood parts to the ¾" (19mm) pine framework. Note that the project has been designed with generous tolerances for all removable parts: The Front and Back pieces, for example, are ¼" (6mm) smaller in width than the opening into which they fit. While some builders might feel uncomfortable leaving such a large tolerance, closer tolerances could result in the Front or Back piece sticking, making it difficult to remove.

Use exterior glue and ⅞" (22mm) wire brads to attach the ¼" (6mm) plywood to the ¾" (19mm) pine cleats.

Drill the cavity holes and vent holes with a Forstner bit to insure clean, splinter-free holes. Cover the vent holes with window screen, stapled in place to the back of the interior walls.

Use hardware cloth with either ¼" (6mm) or ½" (13mm) grids for the flooring on the balconies. Hardware cloth is available in most hardware stores in 36" (915mm)-wide rolls. Use a pair of tin snips to cut it to the size needed.

Hold the Front and Balcony assemblies in place with turn buttons. This makes it extremely easy to remove the assemblies to check on the eggs or the nestlings and to clean the house at the end of the season.

The method of mounting the house on the pole is unique and was designed especially for this project. You will need to purchase a 13' (3962mm)-long piece of 1" (25mm)-diameter steel pipe and 3' (914mm)-long and 4' (1219mm)-long pieces of 1¼" (32mm)-diameter steel pipe. One end of the 3' (914mm) pipe must be threaded so it can be screwed to a 1¼" (32mm) floor flange. The pipe and floor flanges are standard hardware store items. Remember that pipe is measured using the *inside* diameter. **IMPORTANT:** Before purchasing pipe, make sure the 1" (25mm) pipe will slide into the 1¼" (32mm) pipe, as some pipe sizes vary between manufacturers.

The mounting method illustrated in Step 12 shows a 4' (1219mm) length of 1¼" (32mm) pipe buried in the ground. You can use a post-hole digger, set the pipe in straight, and compact around it with gravel (cement optional). Attach the floor flange to the bottom of the house and thread a 3' (914mm) section of 1¼" (32mm) pipe into it. Use a hacksaw or file to cut notches on the exposed end of the 1¼" (32mm) pipe, as shown in Step 12.

Drill the ⁵⁄₁₆" (8mm) holes through where shown on the 13' (3962mm) length of pipe.

Slip one end of the 1" (25mm) pipe up through the 3' (914mm) section of pipe and through the house. Next, slip the other end of the 1" (25mm) pipe into the 1¼" (32mm) pipe in the ground. Raise the house up and place a ¼" (6mm) bolt through the upper hole in the 1" (25mm) pipe. The notch in the 1¼" (32mm) pipes will prevent the house from rotating. **IMPORTANT:** Once martins have started building nests, you must never allow your Martin House to turn, as this can disorientate the martins and prevent them from finding their cavity entrance.

Begin by cutting each of the parts as described below. Then, assemble the project according to the Final Assembly instructions and as shown in the Assembly Drawings.

Purple martins can be identified by their dark purple coloring.

SMALL ROOF: Lay out and cut to size from ¼" (6mm) plywood. Cut the 24-degrees bevel. (Four pieces required.)

LARGE ROOF: Lay out and cut to size from ¼" (6mm) plywood according to the Bill of Materials. (Two pieces required.)

DIVIDER: Lay out and cut to size from ¼" (6mm) plywood according to the Bill of Materials. (Twelve pieces required.)

FLOOR: Lay out and cut to size from ¼" (6mm) plywood. Cut the ⅝" x ⅞" (16 x 22mm) notches in the corners. (Four pieces required.)

FRONT/BACK: Lay out and cut to size from ¼" (6mm) plywood. Drill the 2¼" (57mm)-diameter holes.
TIP: If screech owls are present in your area, reduce the entrance hole to 2" (51mm) in diameter. (Two pieces required.)

WALL: Lay out and cut to size from ¼" (6mm) plywood. Cut the ¾" x ¾" (19 x 19mm) notches in the corners. Drill the 1¼" (32mm)-diameter ventilation holes. (Two pieces required.)

SIDE: Lay out and cut to size from ¼" (6mm) plywood. (Two pieces required.)

BOTTOM: Lay out and cut to size from ¼" (6mm) plywood. Drill the 1⅛" (29mm) vent holes and the 1½" (38mm)-diameter center holes.

BALCONY CLEAT A: Lay out and cut to size from ¾" (19mm) stock. (Sixteen pieces required.)

BALCONY CLEATS B AND C: Lay out and cut to size from ¾" (19mm) stock. (Eight pieces each required.)

DIVIDER CLEATS A AND B: Lay out and cut to size from ¾" (19mm) stock. (Sixteen pieces each required.)

SIDE AND ROOF CLEATS: Lay out and cut to size from ¾" (19mm) stock. (Four pieces each required.)

BOTTOM AND WALL CLEATS: Lay out and cut to size from ¾" (19mm) stock. (Two pieces each required.)

CENTER CLEAT: Lay out and cut to size from ¾" (19mm) stock. (Four pieces required.)

BASE: Lay out and cut to size from ¾" (19mm) stock. Drill the 1½" (38mm)-diameter hole.

SANDING: Finish-sand all parts.

Did you know? A myth has been circulating for years that purple martins will eat up to 3,000 mosquitoes a day. This is not true. Although martins will eat mosquitoes, they prefer larger prey such as dragonflies, mayflies, moths, and butterflies. These larger insects are most apt to be found one hundred feet (thirty meters) or more above ground, much higher than the typical range of mosquitoes. So while martins don't eat as many mosquitoes as some people believe, they do eat hundreds of insects every day.

FINAL ASSEMBLY

STEP 1: Glue and nail the Bottom Cleat, Center Cleat, and Side Cleats to the Side piece in the position shown in the drawing of the Side piece. Note the Bottom Cleat is raised ¼" (6mm) off the bottom edge of the Side piece. (Two assemblies required.)

STEP 2: Attach the Wall Cleats to the Bottom in the position shown on the drawing of the Bottom piece. Staple window screen or hardware cloth to the back side of the Wall pieces over the ventilation holes. Attach the Center Cleats to the Wall pieces in the position shown on the drawing of the Wall piece. Note the Center Cleats are located ¾" (19mm) from the bottom edge of the Wall pieces. Attach the Wall Assembly to the Bottom by nailing it to the Wall Cleats.

STEP 3: Attach the Side assemblies to the Bottom/ Wall assembly.

STEP 4: Attach the Divider Cleat A and Divider Cleat B pieces to the underside of the Floor pieces in the position shown on the drawing of the Floor piece. (Four assemblies required.)

STEP 5: Insert six Dividers and two Floor assemblies. *Do not* glue in place.

STEP 6: Insert the remaining six Dividers and two Floor assemblies. *Do not* glue in place.

STEP 7: Attach the Roof Cleats to the Side pieces. Attach the Large Roof pieces to the Roof Cleats.

STEP 8: Attach the Small Roof pieces to the Center Cleats. Attach the Base to the Bottom. Screw the 1¼" (32mm) pipe flange to the Base.

STEP 9: Assemble two Balcony Cleat A, two Balcony Cleat B, and two Balcony Cleat C pieces as shown. Attach the hardware cloth to the Balcony assembly with nails or staples. (Four assemblies required.)

Attach two Balcony assemblies to the Front/Back piece in the position shown on the drawing of the Front/Back piece. (Two assemblies required.)

STEP 10: Position the Front/Back/Balcony assembly and attach the remaining Balcony Cleat A pieces to the Sides in the position shown on the drawing of the Side piece.

STEP 11: Secure the Front/Back/Balcony assemblies in place with turn buttons.

STEP 12: File a notch in each of the 1¼" (32mm) pieces of pipe as shown. Screw the threaded end of the 3' (914mm) pipe into the floor flange. Drill the ⁵⁄₁₆" (8mm) hole in the upper end of the 1" (25mm) pipe 48" (1220mm) down from the top. Drill the ⁵⁄₁₆" (8mm)-diameter hole through the lower end of the 1" (25mm) pipe, being sure that when you install the bolt it will rest on the notch in the buried piece of 1¼" (32mm) pipe (this distance may be less than 4" (102mm) from the end if dirt has filled in the buried piece of 1¼" (32mm) pipe). Slide the 3" (915mm) length of 1¼" (32mm) pipe over the 1" (25mm) pipe. Insert the 1" (25mm) pipe into the 1¼" (32mm) pipe in the ground. Raise the 1¼" (32mm) pipe and house assembly above the upper ⁵⁄₁₆" (8mm) hole and slip in a ¼" (6mm) bolt and locknut. The bolt will prevent the house from sliding down the pipe and the notch will prevent the wind from rotating the house.

FINISHING: It is best to paint the project with light colors, as this will help keep the house cool. We painted most of the house white, but did paint the Small and Large Roof light green to provide a contrasting color scheme. Do not paint the interior of the house.

WINTER STORAGE: To prevent sparrows from invading the house after the martins have left, you can take the house down and store it indoors.

Bill of Materials

Qty.	Part	Size of Material
4	Small Roof	¼" x 1⅝" x 13¼" (6 x 41 x 337mm)
2	Large Roof	¼" x 15" x 28" (6 x 381 x 711mm) (not drawn)
12	Divider	¼" x 6" x 10⅝" (6 x 152 x 270mm) (not drawn)
4	Floor	¼" x 10⅝" x 23¼" (6 x 270 x 591mm)
2	Front/Back	¼" x 12½" x 21¾" (6 x 318 x 552mm)
2	Wall	¼" x 14" x 23½" (6 x 356 x 597mm)
2	Side	¼" x 18½" x 23¾" (6 x 470 x 603mm)
1	Bottom	¼" x 23½" x 23¾" (6 x 597 x 603mm)
16	Balcony Cleat A	¾" x ¾" x 4½" (19 x 19 x 114mm)
8	Balcony Cleat B	¾" x ¾" x 24" (19 x 19 x 610mm)
8	Balcony Cleat C	¾" x ¾" x 10½" (19 x 19 x 267mm)
16	Divider Cleat A	¾" x ¾" x 4¹³⁄₁₆" (19 x 19 x 122mm)
16	Divider Cleat B	¾" x ¾" x 5½" (19 x 19 x 140mm)
4	Side Cleat	¾" x ¾" x 13⅛" (19 x 19 x 333mm)
4	Roof Cleat	¾" x ¾" x 13⁷⁄₁₆" (19 x 19 x 341mm)
2	Bottom Cleat	¾" x ¾" x 22¼" (19 x 19 x 565mm)
2	Wall Cleat	¾" x 1½" x 3¾" (19 x 38 x 95mm)
4	Center Cleat	¾" x 1½" x 18½" (19 x 38 x 470mm)
1	Base	¾" x 9" (19 x 229mm) diameter
8	Half-Turn Button w/ Screw	1¼" (32mm)
4	½" Hardware Cloth	5½" x 24" (140 x 610mm)
4	Window Screen	9" x 9" (229 x 229mm)
1	Flange w/ Screws	1¼" (32mm)
1	Pipe	13' (3962mm) long; 1" (25mm) interior diameter
1	Pipe	4' (1219mm) long; 1¼" (32mm) interior diameter
1	Pipe	3' (914mm) long; 1¼" (32mm) interior diameter
2	Bolt w/ Locknut	2" (51mm) long; ¼" (6mm) diameter
16	Plastic Plugs (optional)	2¼" (57mm)

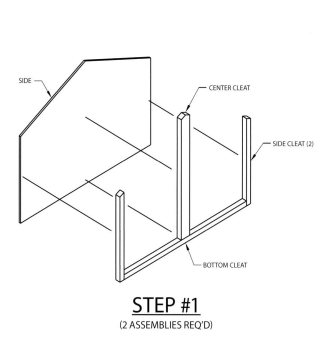

STEP #1
(2 ASSEMBLIES REQ'D)

SIDE

CENTER CLEAT

SIDE CLEAT (2)

BOTTOM CLEAT

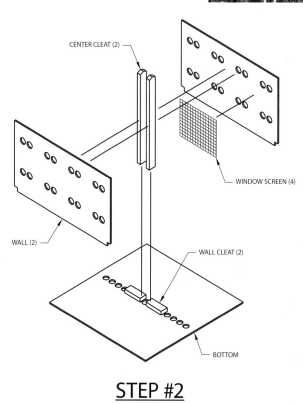

CENTER CLEAT (2)

WINDOW SCREEN (4)

WALL (2)

WALL CLEAT (2)

BOTTOM

STEP #2

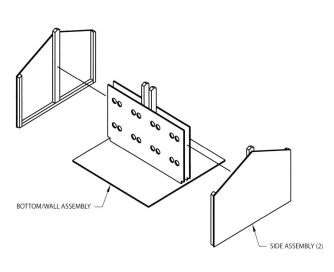

BOTTOM/WALL ASSEMBLY

SIDE ASSEMBLY (2)

STEP #3

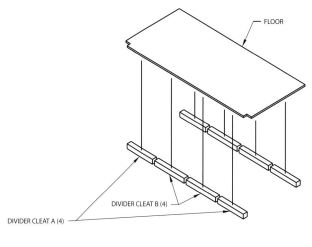

FLOOR

DIVIDER CLEAT B (4)

DIVIDER CLEAT A (4)

STEP #4

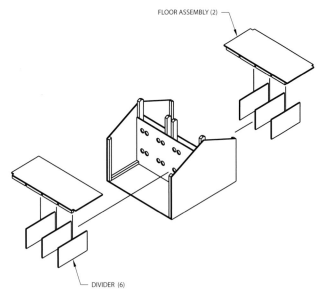

FLOOR ASSEMBLY (2)

DIVIDER (6)

STEP #5

FLOOR ASSEMBLY (2)

DIVIDER (6)

STEP #6

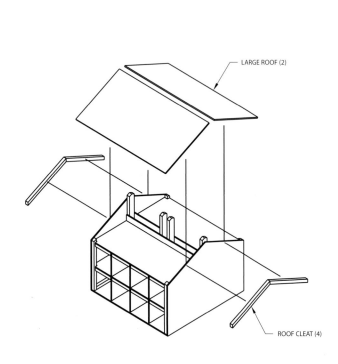

LARGE ROOF (2)

ROOF CLEAT (4)

STEP #7

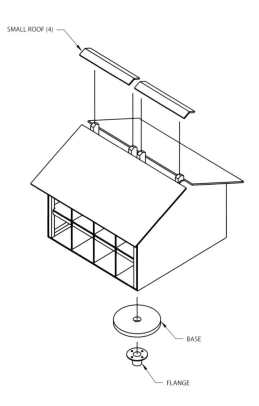

SMALL ROOF (4)

BASE

FLANGE

STEP #8

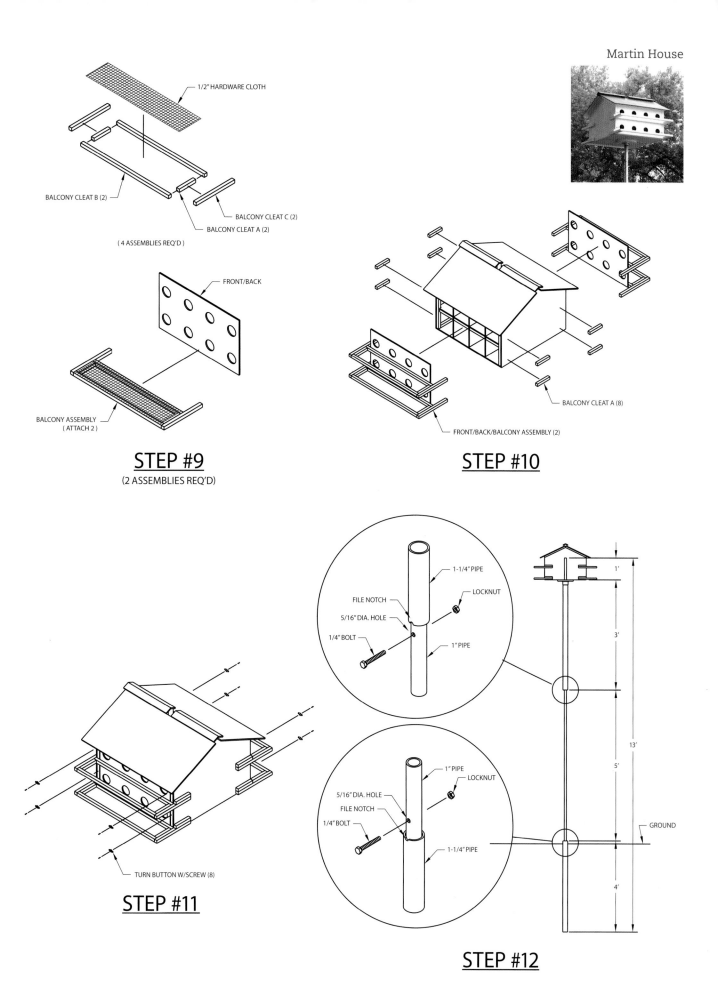

Martin House

1/2" HARDWARE CLOTH

BALCONY CLEAT B (2)

BALCONY CLEAT C (2)

BALCONY CLEAT A (2)

(4 ASSEMBLIES REQ'D)

FRONT/BACK

BALCONY ASSEMBLY
(ATTACH 2)

STEP #9
(2 ASSEMBLIES REQ'D)

BALCONY CLEAT A (8)

FRONT/BACK/BALCONY ASSEMBLY (2)

STEP #10

TURN BUTTON W/SCREW (8)

STEP #11

1-1/4" PIPE

FILE NOTCH

LOCKNUT

5/16" DIA. HOLE

1/4" BOLT

1" PIPE

1" PIPE

LOCKNUT

5/16" DIA. HOLE

FILE NOTCH

1/4" BOLT

1-1/4" PIPE

GROUND

1'

3'

13'

5'

4'

STEP #12

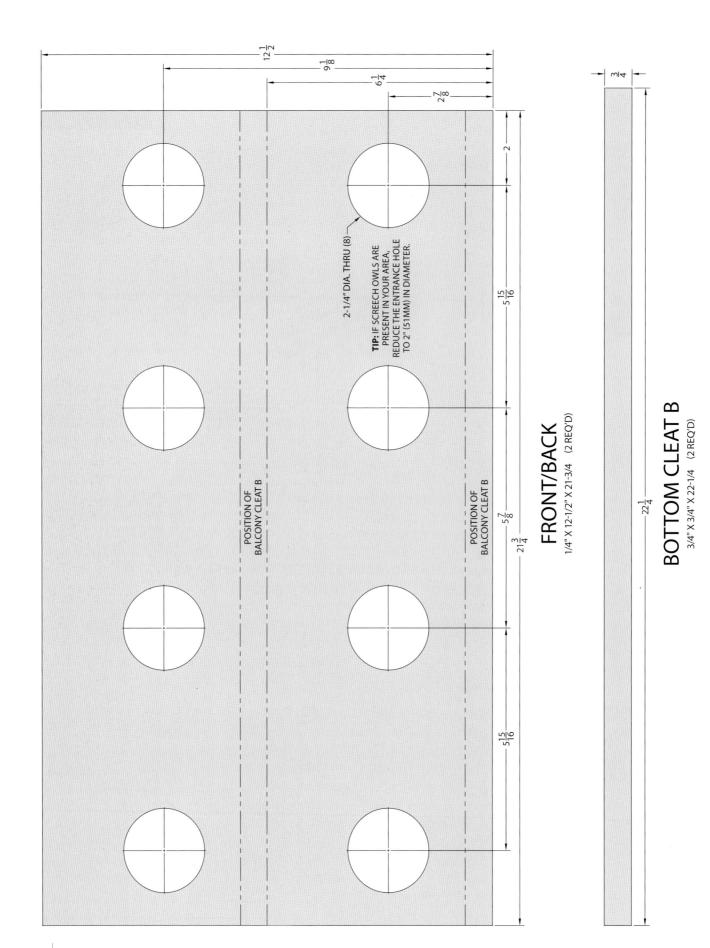

$12\frac{1}{2}$

$9\frac{1}{8}$

$6\frac{1}{4}$

$2\frac{7}{8}$

$\frac{3}{4}$

2

2-1/4" DIA. THRU (8)

TIP: IF SCREECH OWLS ARE PRESENT IN YOUR AREA, REDUCE THE ENTRANCE HOLE TO 2" (51MM) IN DIAMETER.

$5\frac{15}{16}$

POSITION OF BALCONY CLEAT B

POSITION OF BALCONY CLEAT B

$5\frac{7}{8}$

$21\frac{3}{4}$

$5\frac{15}{16}$

FRONT/BACK
1/4" X 12-1/2" X 21-3/4 (2 REQ'D)

$22\frac{1}{4}$

BOTTOM CLEAT B
3/4" X 3/4" X 22-1/4 (2 REQ'D)

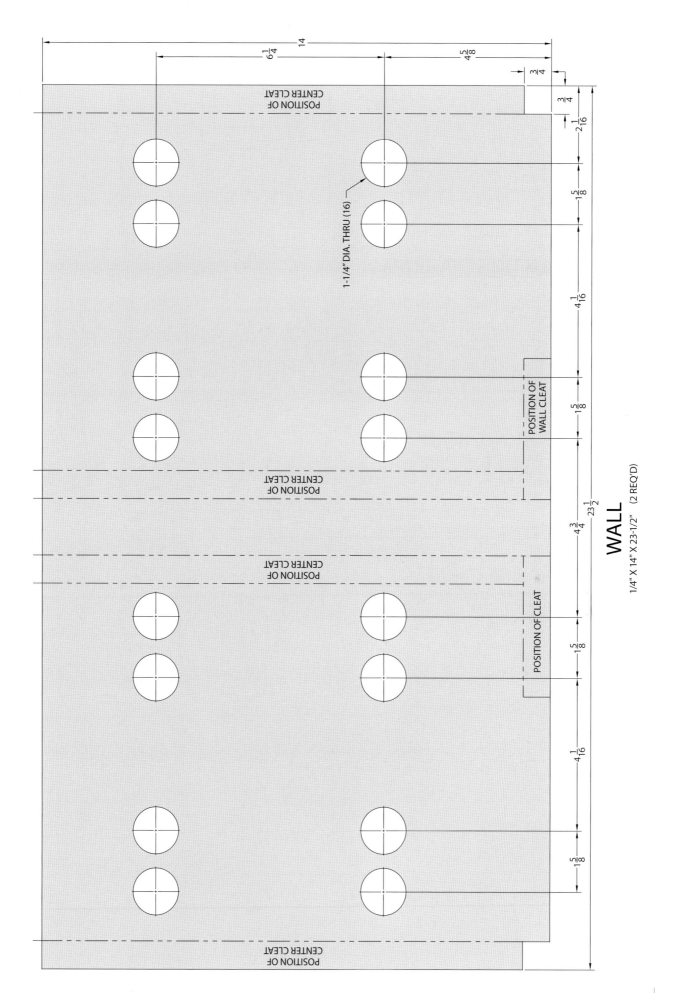

WALL

1/4" X 14" X 23-1/2" (2 REQ'D)

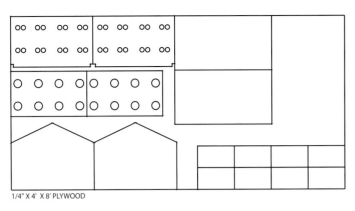
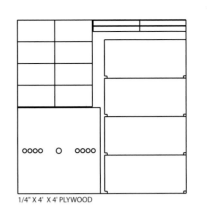

1/4" X 4' X 8' PLYWOOD

1/4" X 4' X 4' PLYWOOD

PLYWOOD CUTTING DIAGRAM

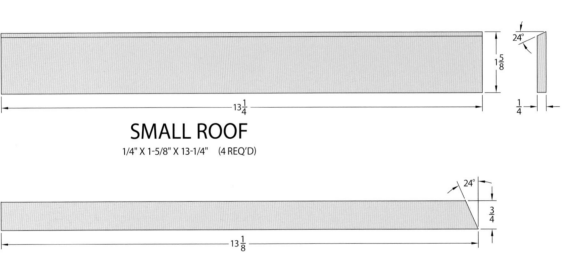

SMALL ROOF
1/4" X 1-5/8" X 13-1/4"   (4 REQ'D)

24°

$13\frac{1}{4}$

$1\frac{5}{8}$

$\frac{1}{4}$

SIDE CLEAT
3/4" X 3/4" X 13-1/8"   (4 REQ'D)

24°

$13\frac{1}{8}$

$\frac{3}{4}$

DIVIDER CLEAT B
3/4" X 3/4" X 5-1/2"   (16 REQ'D)

$5\frac{1}{2}$

$\frac{3}{4}$

POSITION OF
WALL CLEAT

$1\frac{1}{2}$

$3\frac{3}{4}$

WALL CLEAT
3/4" X 1-1/2" X 3-3/4"   (2 REQ'D)

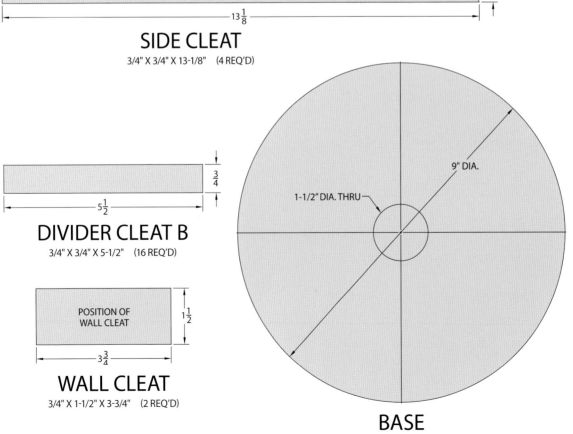

9" DIA.

1-1/2" DIA. THRU

BASE
3/4" X 9" DIA.

$\frac{3}{4}$

24

BALCONY CLEAT B
3/4" X 3/4" X 24"   (8 REQ'D)

Martin House

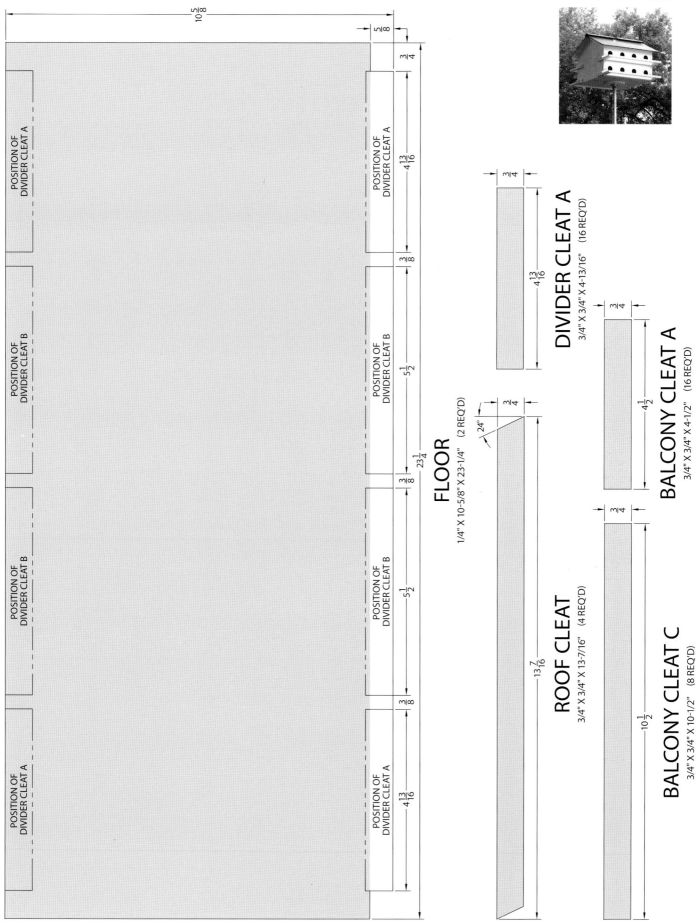

10 5/8

5/8

3/4

POSITION OF DIVIDER CLEAT A

4 13/16

3/8

POSITION OF DIVIDER CLEAT B

5 1/2

3/8

23 1/4

POSITION OF DIVIDER CLEAT B

5 1/2

3/8

POSITION OF DIVIDER CLEAT A

4 13/16

FLOOR
1/4" X 10-5/8" X 23-1/4"   (2 REQ'D)

3/4

24°

13 7/16

ROOF CLEAT
3/4" X 3/4" X 13-7/16"   (4 REQ'D)

3/4

4 13/16

DIVIDER CLEAT A
3/4" X 3/4" X 4-13/16"   (16 REQ'D)

3/4

4 1/2

BALCONY CLEAT A
3/4" X 3/4" X 4-1/2"   (16 REQ'D)

3/4

10 1/2

BALCONY CLEAT C
3/4" X 3/4" X 10-1/2"   (8 REQ'D)

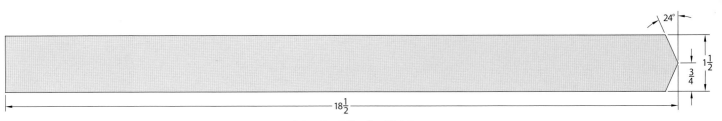

CENTER CLEAT
3/4" X 1-1/2" X 18-1/2"   (4 REQ'D)

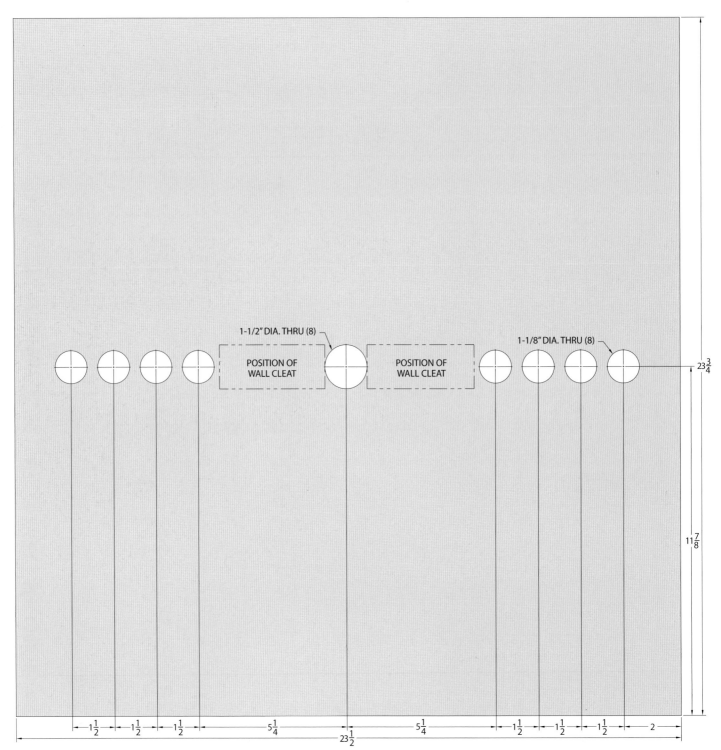

BOTTOM
1/4" X 23-1/2" X 23-3/4"   (4 REQ'D)

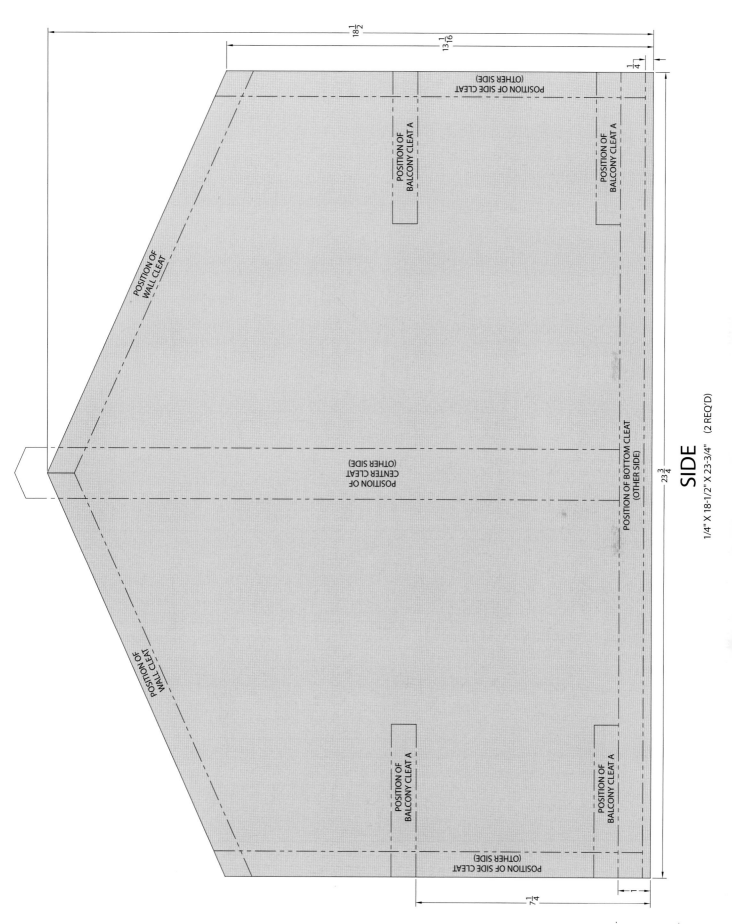

SIDE

1/4" X 18-1/2" X 23-3/4"   (2 REQ'D)

18½

13¹⁄₁₆

¼

POSITION OF SIDE CLEAT
(OTHER SIDE)

POSITION OF
BALCONY CLEAT A

POSITION OF
BALCONY CLEAT A

POSITION OF
WALL CLEAT

POSITION OF BOTTOM CLEAT

POSITION OF
CENTER CLEAT
(OTHER SIDE)

23¾

POSITION OF
WALL CLEAT

POSITION OF
BALCONY CLEAT A

POSITION OF
BALCONY CLEAT A

POSITION OF SIDE CLEAT
(OTHER SIDE)

7¼

Traditional Suet Feeder

Suet is animal fat, usually from cows (beef) or sheep (mutton). It is inexpensive, and some butchers may even give you bulk suet at no charge. The most convenient way to purchase suet, however, is in pre-packaged blocks available from stores that sell bird food.

Suet is high in calories and so provides birds with an important source of energy. In winter, when temperatures are cold, birds have to eat plenty of food to stay warm. The high calories in suet help them stay alive. In the spring and early summer, many birds have just completed a long journey north and must immediately begin defending their territories, mating, building nests, and raising their young. Suet gives them the extra boost they need. In late summer and fall, migrating birds must build up their fat reserves for the long flight. You can see how important it is that you make this vital resource available year around.

This suet feeder design has a long tail extending down from the bottom, serving as a brace for larger birds like the colorful red-headed woodpecker. By pressing their tails against it they can better balance their bodies while they peck at the suet. Besides woodpeckers, you can expect to see many other insect-eating birds visit this bird feeder.

The 4½" x 4½" (114 x 114mm) standard ½" (13mm)-grid hardware cloth (coarse wire screen) is attached to each side to hold the suet block in place. The top, guided by the same rope used to hang the project, lifts straight up, making it easy to refill with a fresh suet block.

The project as pictured was made from cedar boards.

Prepackaged suet blocks can be used with this feeder.

TIP: Save money in the winter by filling your suet feeder with inexpensive raw beef fat from the butcher shop. But in the hotter months raw fat can melt and get rancid. In hot climates it's best to switch to commercially rendered suet cakes. The rendering (boiling) process kills bacteria.

How-To Instructions

This project is constructed from ¾" (19mm) lumber. It is pictured in cedar, but pine or another wood can be used. Assembly is completed with nails and screws. Where screws are used, the screw hole locations are shown on the drawings.

SCREEN MOUNT: Lay out and cut to size from ¾" (19mm) stock. Drill the 1" (25mm)-diameter hole through. (Two pieces required.)

BOTTOM: Lay out and cut to size from ¾" (19mm) stock. Drill the 9/64" (3.6mm)-diameter holes through and countersink for screws.

SIDE AND TOP: Lay out and cut to size from ¾" (19mm) stock. Drill the ½" (13mm)-diameter hole through for the rope. (Two pieces each required.)

SUPPORT: Lay out and cut to size from ¾" (19mm) stock.

HARDWARE CLOTH: Use tin snips to cut two 6" x 8" (152 x 203mm) pieces of ½" (13mm)-square hardware cloth.

SANDING: Finish-sand all parts.

CLEAT: Lay out and cut to size from ¾" (19mm) stock. (Two pieces required.)

Cut the parts as described below. Then, assemble the project according to the Final Assembly instructions and as shown in the Assembly Drawing.

FINAL ASSEMBLY

STEP 1: Glue and screw the Support to the Bottom using #6 2" (51mm) screws. Glue and nail the Bottom and Screen Mount pieces to the Sides where shown.

STEP 2: Attach the Cleats to the Sides where shown. Attach the hardware cloth to the Screen Mount pieces with staples or nails. Attach the Top as follows: Each end of the rope is pushed through one of the holes in the Top piece and then through one of the holes in the nearest Side piece. Tie a knot on each end of the rope. The knots will be on the inside of the feeder. You will be able to simply lift the Top piece for refilling without having to tie or untie the rope.

FINISHING: All cedar parts were left unfinished.

Bill of Materials

Qty.	Part	Size of Material
2	Cleat	¾" x 1¼" x 7½" (19 x 32 x 191mm)
2	Screen Mount	¾" x 1½" x 8" (19 x 38 x 203mm)
1	Bottom	¾" x 2¼" x 6" (19 x 57 x 152mm)
2	Side	¾" x 2¼" x 8¾" (19 x 57 x 222mm)
1	Top	¾" x 3¾" x 9½" (19 x 95 x 241mm)
1	Support	¾" x 4½" x 14" (19 x 114 x 356mm)
1	Rope	⅜" (10mm) diameter; 6' (1829mm) long
4	#6 Screw	2" (51mm)
1	½" (13mm)-Grid Hardware Cloth	8" x 12" (203 x 305mm)

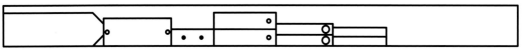

1" X 6" X 6'

CUTTING DIAGRAM

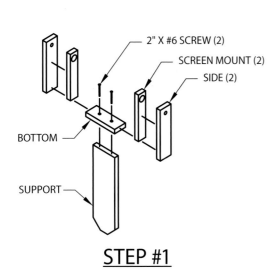

2" X #6 SCREW (2)

SCREEN MOUNT (2)

SIDE (2)

BOTTOM

SUPPORT

STEP #1

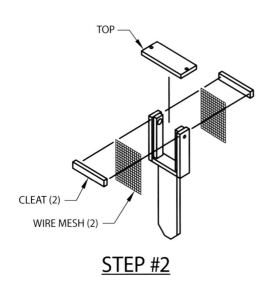

TOP

CLEAT (2)

WIRE MESH (2)

STEP #2

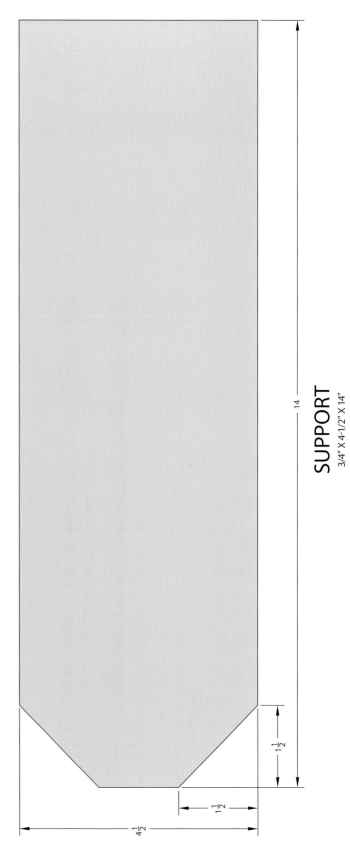

SUPPORT

3/4" X 4-1/2" X 14"

14

$1\frac{1}{2}$

$1\frac{1}{2}$

$4\frac{1}{2}$

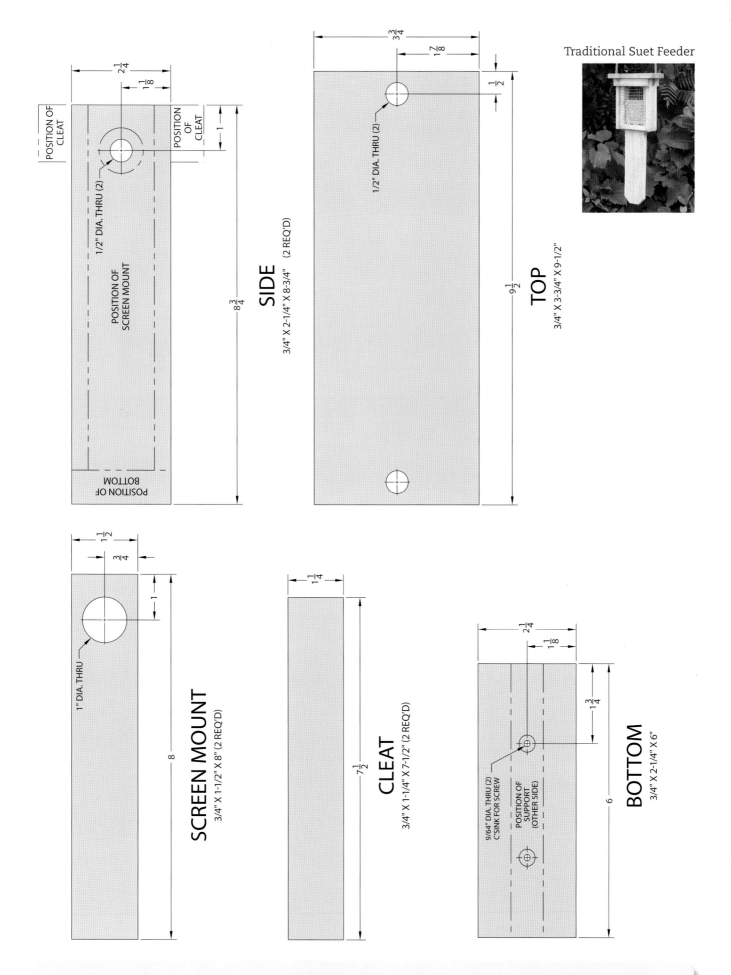

SIDE
3/4" X 2-1/4" X 8-3/4" (2 REQ'D)

POSITION OF CLEAT

1/2" DIA. THRU (2)

POSITION OF SCREEN MOUNT

POSITION OF CLEAT

POSITION OF BOTTOM

2 1/4

1 1/8

1

8 3/4

TOP
3/4" X 3-3/4" X 9-1/2"

3 3/4

1 7/8

1/2

1/2" DIA. THRU (2)

9 1/2

Traditional Suet Feeder

SCREEN MOUNT
3/4" X 1-1/2" X 8" (2 REQ'D)

1 1/2

3/4

1

1" DIA. THRU

8

CLEAT
3/4" X 1-1/4" X 7-1/2" (2 REQ'D)

1 1/4

7 1/2

BOTTOM
3/4" X 2-1/4" X 6"

2 1/4

1 1/8

1 3/4

9/64" DIA. THRU (2)
C'SINK FOR SCREW

POSITION OF SUPPORT (OTHER SIDE)

6

TIP: If starlings take over your suet feeder, try building a feeder with access only from the bottom. Starlings prefer not to perch upside down. Chickadees and woodpeckers do not find this to be a problem, however.

Underside Suet Feeder

In addition to providing several seed feeders, it is important to have at least one or two suet feeders in your yard. Birds that prefer insects are the ones you can expect to show up at your suet feeder. An added bonus to attracting these birds is that you may notice fewer annoying insects when there are frequent visitors to your suet feeder.

Most insect-eating birds devour suet because it is such an excellent source of energy. This food source is especially important in winter, when insects are hard to find. Although birds require this valuable energy source year round, don't hang this feeder in the hot summer sun, as heat can spoil the suet.

This feeder has a 5½" x 5½" (140 x 140mm) suet cavity designed to hold packaged suet blocks available from dealers selling bird food.

With this feeder, the suet is accessed from the underside. This poses no problem for woodpeckers, nuthatches, and chickadees, but discourages less acrobatic birds such as crows and starlings that would otherwise annihilate the suet in short order.

Prepackaged suet blocks can be used with this feeder.

How-To Instructions

This project is constructed from ¾" (19mm) lumber. It is pictured in pine with a cedar-colored stain. If you make it from cedar, you can omit putting on any finish and let the wood age naturally. The Cutting Diagram shows how much lumber you will need. Assembly can be done with water-resistant glue and nails or screws.

Hang the feeder with chain by adding two screw eyes in the position shown on the drawing of the Top piece. Alternatively, hang the feeder by drilling two holes in the Top piece and slipping a rope through them. If using the latter method, be sure to drill the holes so they go inside the cavity so you can tie knots in the ends.

This project requires a coarse wire screen called hardware cloth, with a ½" (13mm) weave. It is available in most hardware stores.

Begin by cutting each of the parts as described below. Then, assemble the project according to the Final Assembly instructions and as shown in the Assembly Drawing.

TOP: Lay out and cut to size from ¾" (19mm) stock. Cut the 22½-degree bevels. If using screw eyes to hang the project, drill screw eye pilot holes where shown.

LID: Lay out and cut to size from ¾" (19mm) stock. Cut the 22½-degree bevel. (Two pieces required.)

SIDE, FRONT, AND BACK: Lay out and cut to size from ¾" (19mm) stock. (Two pieces each required.)

HARDWARE CLOTH: Use tin snips to cut a 6¼" x 6¼" (159 x 159mm) piece of ½" (13mm)-grid hardware cloth.

SANDING: Finish-sand all parts.

FINAL ASSEMBLY

Attach the Front and Back pieces to the Side pieces where shown. Attach the Top to the Front and Back assembly where shown. Rout a ⅜"-wide-by-⅛"-deep (10mm by 3mm) rabbet around the inside of the bottom of the assembly for the hardware cloth. Attach one Lid to the Top with the hinges. The remaining Lid can be permanently fastened in place.

Fasten the hardware cloth to the bottom of the project with staples.

Insert the screw eyes or rope to hang the completed project.

FINISHING: If you make this project from cedar, omit using any type of wood finish and let the wood weather to a natural silver-gray color. You can also brush on a coat of exterior wood preservative or a coat of sanding sealer followed by a coat of exterior polyurethane.

TIP: One of the joys of feeding birds is being able to watch them. When deciding where to place your feeder, pick a location that is convenient to get to, but also a location where you can enjoy watching the birds that come to your feeder. Some suggestions: outside a kitchen window or the sliding glass door leading to a deck.

Bill of Materials

Qty.	Part	Size of Material
1	Top	¾" x 3⅛" x 8½" (19 x 79 x 216mm)
2	Lid	¾" x 5¼" x 8½" (19 x 133 x 216mm)
2	Side	¾" x 1½" x 5½" (19 x 38 x 140mm)
2	Front/Back	¾" x 3¾" x 7" (19 x 95 x 178mm)
2	Screw Eye	1⁹⁄₁₆" (40mm)
1 pair	Hinge w/ Screw	1½" (38mm)
1	½" (13mm)-Grid Hardware Cloth	8" x 12" (203 x 305mm)

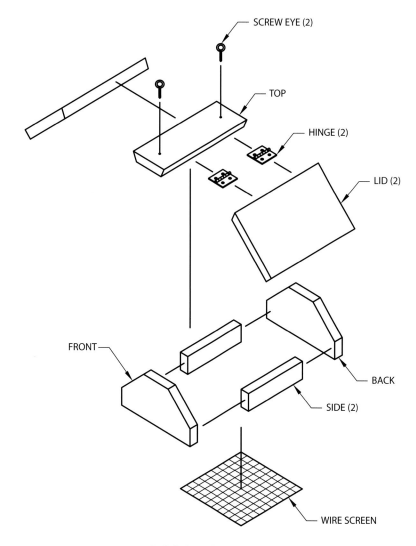

ASSEMBLY DRAWING

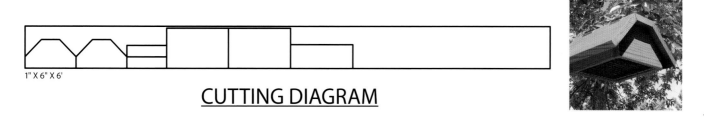

1" X 6" X 6'

CUTTING DIAGRAM

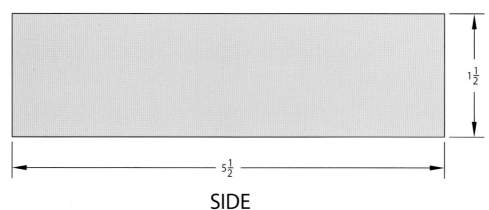

$1\frac{1}{2}$

$5\frac{1}{2}$

SIDE

3/4" X 1-1/2" X 5-1/2"   (2 REQ'D)

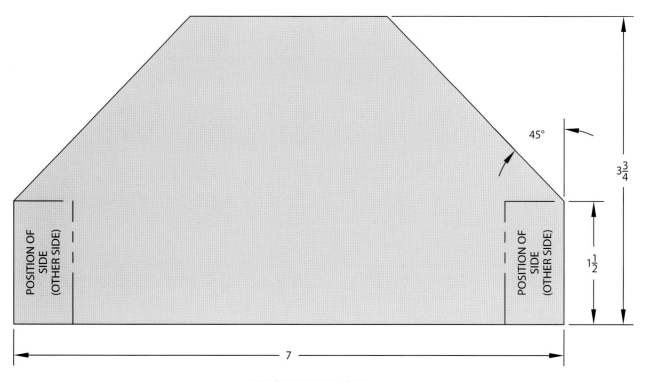

45°

$3\frac{3}{4}$

$1\frac{1}{2}$

POSITION OF
SIDE
(OTHER SIDE)

POSITION OF
SIDE
(OTHER SIDE)

7

FRONT/BACK

3/4" X 3-3/4" X 7"   (2 REQ'D)

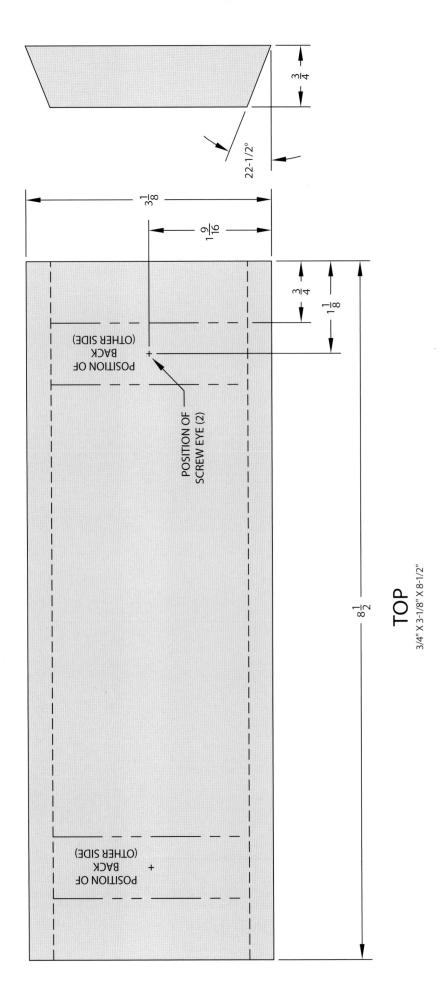

TOP

3/4" X 3-1/8" X 8-1/2"

22-1/2°

3/8 (3⅛)

1 9/16

3/4

1 1/8

8 1/2

3/4

POSITION OF
BACK
(OTHER SIDE)

POSITION OF
SCREW EYE (2)

POSITION OF
BACK
(OTHER SIDE)

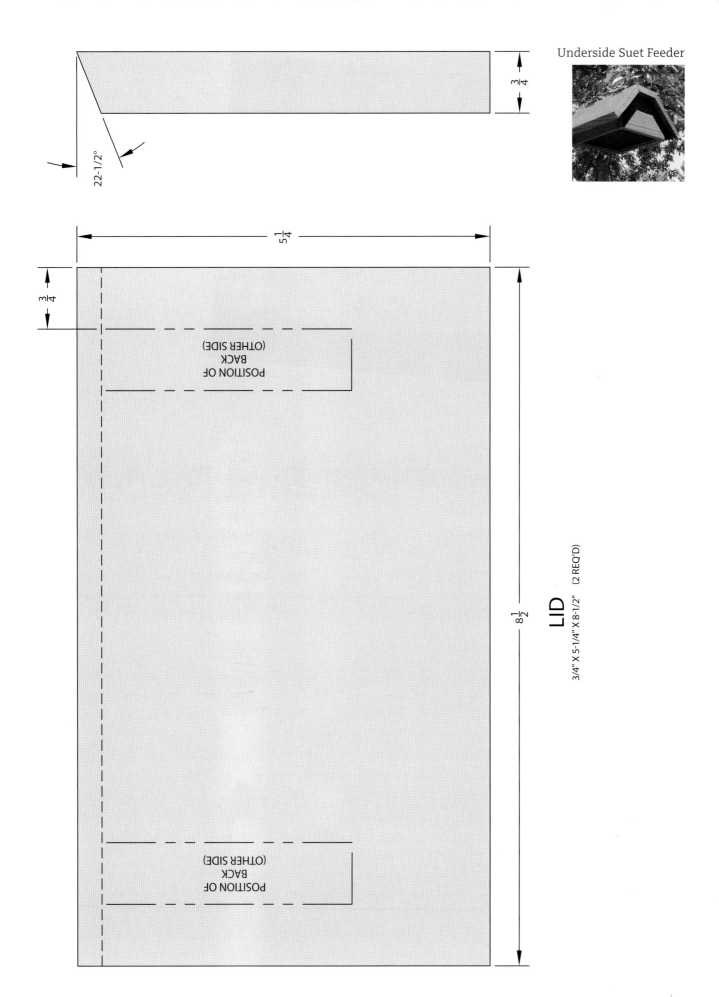

Underside Suet Feeder

3/4

22-1/2°

5 1/4

3/4

POSITION OF
BACK
(OTHER SIDE)

POSITION OF
BACK
(OTHER SIDE)

8 1/2

LID

3/4" X 5-1/4" X 8-1/2"   (2 REQ'D)

Squirrel-Proof Bird Feeder

The original idea behind this specialized type of bird feeder was to foil pesky squirrels, preventing them from stealing the seeds intended for song birds. This easy-to-build feeder works on a simple balance beam. When a squirrel sits on the perch, its weight causes the perch to drop down, sealing off access to the seeds. The counter balance can be adjusted to prevent nuisance birds like starlings and blackbirds from robbing the seed, too.

In reality, the term *squirrel-proof* may be a little optimistic. Squirrels are clever, especially when it comes to cracking the secrets of robbing food from bird feeders; it may not be possible to design a truly 100 percent squirrel-proof feeder. When I first put this feeder in my backyard, I purposely located it where squirrels could jump to it from a nearby tree. My wife and I laughed as we watched the first squirrel jump on the feeder only to discover the platform slammed down, hiding away the seeds. It seemed, at first, that we had outsmarted the troublesome squirrels. After a few weeks, however, we watched an especially agile squirrel use his hind legs to hang from the top, then twist his body in such a way that he could paw out some food without putting pressure on the platform.

The question became how to make a feeder truly squirrel-proof?

The answer was simple enough. I just moved it away from the tree, as should be done with any bird feeder. And, of course, put a metal predator guard on the post.

But why go through the effort of making a birdfeeder with a drop platform if you place the feeder where the squirrels can't possibly reach it anyway? The answer is the whole exercise is worth it for a different reason than you might expect. We found this feeder is a perfect way to keep heavy birds from hogging all the food. The feeder allows several small birds to feed at one time. But when heavy birds like blue jays arrive, they scare away the small birds and eat a great deal of the food themselves, often throwing much of it out of the feeder to get at the sunflower seeds. I've set the counterbalance so a single blue jay or similar heavy bird can enjoy eating, but when a second bird arrives, the platform drops, shutting off the food supply. After four years, the blue jays have not learned the secret of going one at a time, but a single blue jay can access the seed.

How-To Instructions

This project is constructed from ¼" (6mm) and ⅞" (22mm) cedar that is cut, sanded, and glued together. The Stop piece is the only piece specified at ¼" (6mm) thickness. Use a table saw or band saw to re-saw this piece from the ⅞" (22mm) cedar board. Cedar is available in most lumber yards surfaced smooth on one side and left rough on the other side. We faced the rough side out wherever possible, although that is simply our preference. If you prefer to use ¾" (6mm)-thick lumber, it will be necessary to adjust some measurements.

Use standard screen-door hooks to hold the hinged top securely closed, while still making it easy to open for refilling. Complete assembly using exterior glue and nails, except where screws are specified.

Attach the Counterbalance A and B assemblies to the Perch Side pieces with two screws. To fine-tune the balance, remove those screws and move the Counterbalance assembly closer to the feeder or further away from the feeder and reattach screws.

A good way to mount the feeder is with a plumber's floor flange and a piece of ¾" (19mm) galvanized water pipe threaded at one end. Attach a floor flange to the bottom of the project with wood screws. Mount the pipe in the location desired and screw the floor flange to the threads on the top end of the pipe.

This plan includes drawings for all parts except those that are a simple rectangular shape. The dimensions of all pieces are given in the Bill of Materials. For those pieces designated in the Bill of Materials as "not drawn," simply cut them to the width and length given.

Begin by cutting each of the parts as described below. Then, assemble the project according to the Final Assembly instructions and as shown in the Assembly Drawing.

The weight of the squirrel closes off access to the seed.

TIP: Expect squirrels to try to reach your feeder. Hanging a feeder from a tree limb is like an invitation to squirrels. Once they gain access, they will take over the feeder, eat the seed, and scare away the birds. The best way to keep squirrels out is to mount the feeder on a steel pipe and attach a metal squirrel guard to the pole. Make sure it is at least 8' (2438mm) from any trees, as squirrels can jump great distances.

STOP: Lay out and cut to size from ¼" (6mm) cedar. Drill the 9⁄64" (3.6mm)-diameter screw clearance holes through and countersink for screws.

PERCH: Lay out and cut to size from ⅞" (22mm) cedar stock according to the dimensions given in the Bill of Materials. (Four pieces required.)

PERCH SIDE: Lay out and cut to size from ⅞" (22mm) cedar stock. Drill the 9⁄64" (3.6mm)-diameter screw clearance holes through and countersink for screws. (Two pieces required.)

STOP SUPPORT: Lay out and cut to size from ⅞" (22mm) cedar stock according to the dimensions given in the Bill of Materials. (Two pieces required.)

COUNTERBALANCE A: Lay out and cut to size from ⅞" (22mm) cedar stock according to the dimensions given in the Bill of Materials. Drill the 9⁄64" (3.6mm) screw clearance holes 15⁄16" (24mm) from each end and centered from side to side. Countersink for screws.

COUNTERBALANCE B: Lay out and cut to size from ⅞" (22mm) cedar stock according to the dimensions given in the Bill of Materials. Drill the 9⁄64" (3.6mm) screw clearance holes 2" (51mm) from each end and centered from side to side. Countersink for screws.

FEEDER SIDE: Lay out and cut to size from ⅞" (22mm) cedar stock. Drill the 7⁄64" (2.8mm)-diameter screw pilot hole through. (One right-hand and one left-hand piece required.)

ROOF A: Lay out and cut to size from ⅞" (22mm) cedar stock. Cut the bevel as shown.

FRONT, BACK, BOTTOM, LIP, AND ROOF B: Lay out and cut to size from ⅞" (22mm) cedar stock according to the dimensions given in the Bill of Materials.

CHUTE: Lay out and cut to size from ⅞" (22mm) cedar stock. Cut the bevels as shown. To cut the 50-degree bevel, tilt your table saw blade to 40 degrees, position the Chute piece as shown in Detail A, clamp a board to the Chute piece to act as a guide, and then cut the bevel. The guide will slide along the rip fence as you make the cut. Because the Chute piece must be in the vertical position when you cut the bevel, this guide will provide a safe way to cut the bevel.

SANDING: Finish-sand all parts.

FINAL ASSEMBLY

STEP 1: Attach the outer two Perch pieces and Stop Support pieces to the Perch Sides with the #6 2" (51mm) screws where shown. Nail the remaining Perch pieces in place.

STEP 2: Attach the Stop to the Stop Support pieces with #6 1¼" (32mm) screws where shown. Attach the Counterbalance B to the Counterbalance A with the #6 1¼" (32mm) screws. Attach the Counterbalance A/B assembly to the Perch Sides with the #6 1¼" (32mm) screws.

STEP 3: Glue and nail the Front, Back, Bottom, and Chute pieces to the Feeder Side pieces centered and in the position shown on the drawing of the Perch Side piece. Glue and nail the Lip to the Feeder Sides where shown.

STEP 4: Glue and nail the Roof A piece to the Feeder Side pieces centered and in the position shown on the drawing of the Perch Side piece. Attach the hinges to the Roof B piece 2¼" (57mm) from each end and flush with the bottom edge. Position Roof B and screw the hinges to the Back piece. Attach the hook and screw eyes to the Roof B and Feeder Side pieces to secure.

STEP 5: Attach the Perch Sides to the Feeder Sides with the #6 2" (51mm) screws and washers. Mount the finished project with a floor flange and steel pipe.

FINISHING: All cedar pieces were left unfinished.

Bill of Materials

Qty.	Part	Size of Material
1	Stop	¼" x 2¼" x 12¼" (6 x 57 x 311mm)
4	Perch	⅞" x 1" x 10½" (22 x 25 x 267mm) (not drawn)
2	Perch Side	⅞" x 1" x 21" (22 x 25 x 533mm)
2	Stop Support	⅞" x 2" x 4" (22 x 51 x 102mm) (not drawn)
1	Counterbalance A	⅞" x 5½" x 13¼" (22 x 140 x 337mm) (not drawn)
1	Counterbalance B	⅞" x 5½" x 10½" (22 x 140 x 267mm) (not drawn)
2	Feeder Side	⅞" x 5¼" x 7⁵⁄₁₆" (22 x 133 x 186mm)
1	Front	⅞" x 3⅞" x 8½" (22 x 133 x 216mm) (not drawn)
1	Back	⅞" x 6¼" x 8½" (22 x 159 x 216mm) (not drawn)
1	Bottom	⅞" x 4⅜" x 8½" (22 x 111 x 216mm) (not drawn)
1	Chute	⅞" x 5⁷⁄₁₆" x 8½" (22 x 138 x 216mm) (not drawn)
1	Lip	⅞" x 1⅜" x 10¼" (22 x 35 x 260mm) (not drawn)
1	Roof A	⅞" x 4⅞" x 12¼" (22 x 124 x 311mm)
1	Roof B	⅞" x 7" x 12¼" (22 x 178 x 311mm) (not drawn)
2	Washer	1" (25mm) outer diameter; ¼" (6mm) Inner diameter
8	#6 Screw	1¼" (32mm)
10	#6 Screw	2" (51mm)
1 pair	Hinge w/ Screws	1½" (38mm)
1	Hook w/ Screw Eye	1½" (38mm)

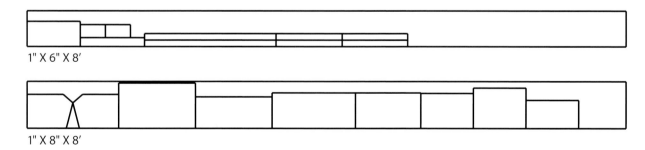

1" X 6" X 8'

1" X 8" X 8'

CUTTING DIAGRAM

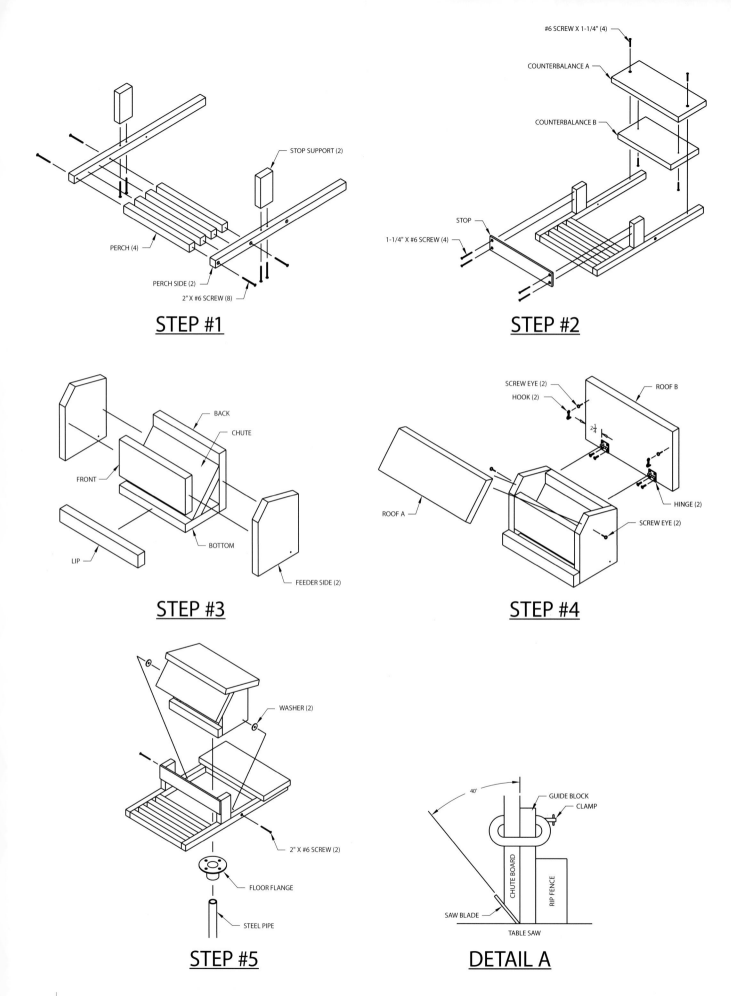

STOP SUPPORT (2)

PERCH (4)

PERCH SIDE (2)

2" X #6 SCREW (8)

STEP #1

#6 SCREW X 1-1/4" (4)

COUNTERBALANCE A

COUNTERBALANCE B

STOP

1-1/4" X #6 SCREW (4)

STEP #2

BACK

CHUTE

FRONT

LIP

BOTTOM

FEEDER SIDE (2)

STEP #3

SCREW EYE (2)

HOOK (2)

ROOF B

$2\frac{1}{4}$

ROOF A

HINGE (2)

SCREW EYE (2)

STEP #4

WASHER (2)

2" X #6 SCREW (2)

FLOOR FLANGE

STEEL PIPE

STEP #5

40°

GUIDE BLOCK

CLAMP

CHUTE BOARD

RIP FENCE

SAW BLADE

TABLE SAW

DETAIL A

Squirrel-Proof Bird Feeder

40°

50°

$5\frac{7}{16}$

$8\frac{1}{2}$

$\frac{7}{8}$

CHUTE
7/8" X 5-7/16" X 8-1/2"

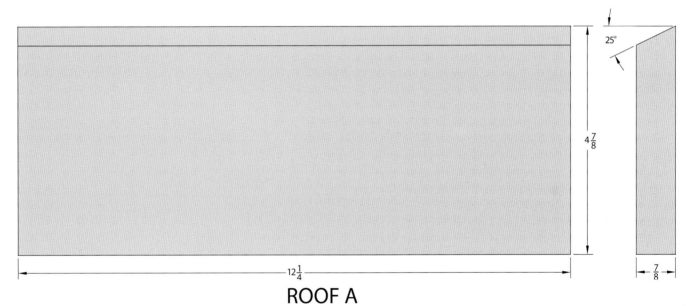

25°

$4\frac{7}{8}$

$12\frac{1}{4}$

$\frac{7}{8}$

ROOF A
7/8" X 4-7/8" X 12-1/4"

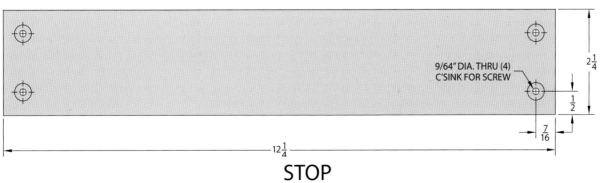

9/64" DIA. THRU (4)
C'SINK FOR SCREW

$2\frac{1}{4}$

$\frac{1}{2}$

$\frac{7}{16}$

$12\frac{1}{4}$

STOP
1/4" X 2-1/4" X 12-1/4"

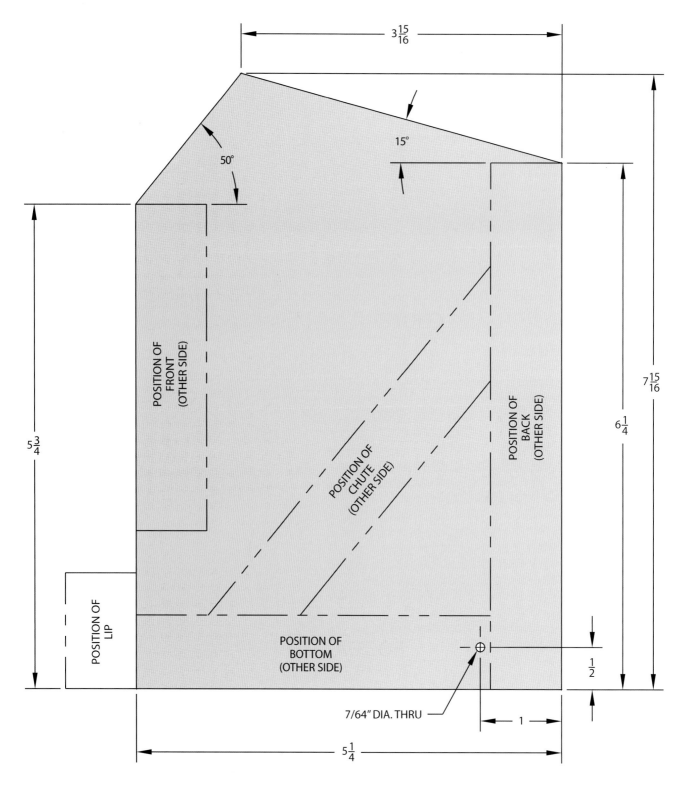

$3\frac{15}{16}$

15°

50°

POSITION OF
FRONT
(OTHER SIDE)

POSITION OF
CHUTE
(OTHER SIDE)

POSITION OF
BACK
(OTHER SIDE)

$5\frac{3}{4}$

$7\frac{15}{16}$

$6\frac{1}{4}$

POSITION OF
LIP

POSITION OF
BOTTOM
(OTHER SIDE)

7/64" DIA. THRU

$\frac{1}{2}$

1

$5\frac{1}{4}$

FEEDER SIDE

7/8" X 5-1/4" X 7-5/16"   (1 RH & 1 LH REQ'D)   (RH SHOWN)

TIP: You should also provide a birdbath, which is integral to any preservation effort because birds need water for drinking and bathing. Bathing helps with parasite control and feather maintenance. In winter, especially in cold climates where usual water sources become frozen, an electric water heater will keep the water in a birdbath open and accessible to your backyard visitors. These small heaters take little electricity and are essential to avian survival.

Squirrel-Proof Bird Feeder

POSITION OF COUNTERBALANCE A

POSITION OF COUNTERBALANCE B (OTHER SIDE)

POSITION OF HINGE

POSITION OF ROOF B

POSITION OF FEEDER SIDE

POSITION OF ROOF A

POSITION OF STOP SUPPORT

POSITION OF STOP

9/64" DIA. THRU (D) C'SINK FOR SCREW

9/64" DIA. THRU (2) (ON CENTER) C'SINK FOR SCREW

$\frac{1}{2}$

21

1

$7\frac{1}{4}$

$5\frac{1}{4}$

$7\frac{1}{4}$

POSITION OF PERCH (OTHER SIDE)

$\frac{7}{8}$

$\frac{7}{16}$

$\frac{1}{2}$

PERCH SIDE

7/8" X 1" X 21" (1 RH & 1 LH REQ'D) (RH SHOWN)

Oriole Wishing Well Feeder

Orioles are one of the most colorful birds in North America. It's always a welcome sight to see one land on your feeder. The male is especially beautiful, with his brilliant orange and black body and black head. The female too is colorful. She is olive brown on top and burnt orange and yellow on her underside. Those of us who live in the northern states look forward to seeing the first oriole, as their appearance signals the coming of spring.

The oriole is Maryland's official state bird and the namesake of the state's Major League Baseball team, the Baltimore Orioles. Orioles eat caterpillars and other insects, but they like fruits and nectars as well. They are attracted to backyard feeders with oranges, grape jelly, or peanut butter.

This feeder is designed to look like a miniature wishing well. A 2½" (64mm) finishing nail on each side holds a slice of an orange. Wood perches are positioned below and to each side of the fruit. A 2¼" (57mm) dish-shaped plastic plug holds jelly or peanut butter.

How-To Instructions

This project is made from a ⅝" x 5½" x 6' (16 x 140 x 1829mm) cedar fence board, which keeps building costs low. You can substitute standard ¾" (19mm) boards with minor modifications.

Pre-drill a 1/16" (2mm) hole on each side for the finishing nail. After driving each nail in, use pliers to bend the last ½" (13mm) slightly upward to help keep the orange slice you'll put there later from falling off.

The five Well pieces are identical in size, but drill the top two through with a 2¼" (57mm) Forstner bit to fit the plastic plug specified. Also, drill and countersink the top Well piece so it can be screwed to the middle section (the piece marked Front).

Suspend the finished project from a rope or chain by putting a screw eye in the top of the feeder.

Begin by cutting each of the parts as described below. Then, assemble the project according to the Final Assembly instructions and as shown in the Assembly Drawing.

ROOF A AND ROOF B: Lay out and cut to size from ⅝" (16mm) stock.

FRONT: Lay out and cut to size from ⅝" (16mm) stock. Drill the 1/16" (2mm)-diameter nail pilot holes ½" (13mm) deep. These holes are offset from one another. Drill the ¼" (6mm)-diameter holes through. Drill the 9/64" (3.6mm)-diameter screw pilot holes ⅞" (22mm) deep.

WELL: Lay out and cut five pieces to size from ⅝" (16mm) stock. On the top piece only, drill the 11/64" (4.4mm)-diameter screw clearance holes through and countersink for screws. On the top two pieces, drill the 2¼" (57mm)-diameter hole through. (Five pieces required.)

DOWEL: Lay out and cut to length from ¼" (6mm) dowel stock according to the size given in the Bill of Materials. (Two pieces required.)

SANDING: Finish-sand all parts.

FINAL ASSEMBLY

Attach the top Well piece to the bottom of the Front piece with two wood screws. Rotate the second Well piece and glue and nail to the first. Repeat with remaining Well pieces.

Attach the Roof A and Roof B pieces to the Front piece. Insert the dowels through the ¼" (6mm) holes, center them, and glue in place. If the dowels appear loose, use a small wire brad to pin them.

Pound a 2½" (64mm) nail on each side of the Front and bend up the heads to hold the orange halves. Place the 2¼" (57mm) plastic plug in the base to hold jelly.

The finished project may be suspended from a chain or rope or mounted on a post or deck railing.

FINISHING: If you make this project from cedar, you can omit using any type of wood finish and just let the wood weather to a natural silver gray color. You could also brush a coat of exterior wood preservative or a coat of sanding sealer followed by a coat of exterior polyurethane.

TIP: If you are new to the hobby of feeding birds, start by purchasing blends of wild bird food mixes that will attract the widest variety of species. This way, you will be able to see which species of birds come to your feeder. As you study their habits, you will see some birds are more aggressive than others, like sparrows, starlings, and some black birds. Eventually you may decide you want to attract only certain species. You can do so by switching to seeds specific to the species you prefer. For example, by filling your feeder with safflower seeds, you can expect blue jays and cardinals, but few other species.

Bill of Materials

Qty.	Part	Size of Material
1	Roof A	⅝" x 4⅜" x 5¼" (16 x 111 x 133mm)
1	Roof B	⅝" x 5" x 5¼" (16 x 127 x 133mm)
1	Front	⅝" x 5¼" x 9¾" (16 x 133 x 248mm)
5	Well	⅝" x 5¼" x 5¼" (16 x 133 x 133)
2	Dowel	¼" (6 mm) diameter; 5" (127mm) long
2	Finishing or Casing Nail	2½" (64mm)
2	#8 Wood Screw	1½" (38mm)
1	Plastic Plug	2¼" (57mm)
1	Screw Eye	1⁹⁄₁₆" (40mm)

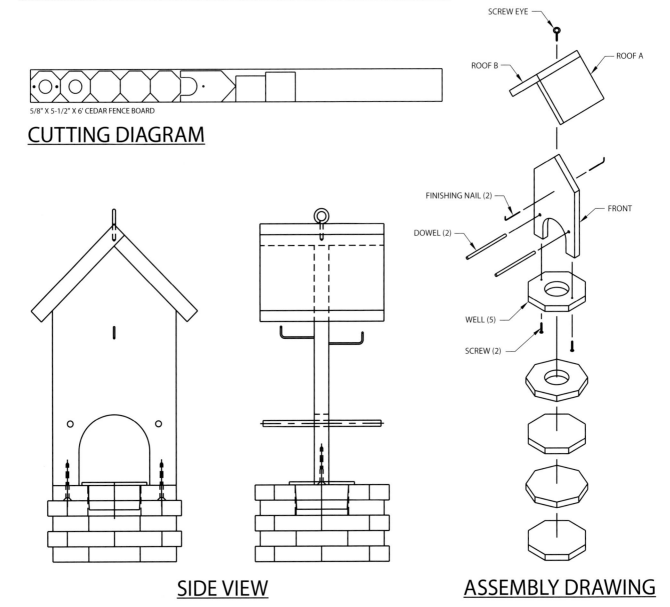

5/8" X 5-1/2" X 6' CEDAR FENCE BOARD

CUTTING DIAGRAM

SIDE VIEW

ASSEMBLY DRAWING

SCREW EYE

ROOF B — ROOF A

FINISHING NAIL (2)

DOWEL (2)

FRONT

WELL (5)

SCREW (2)

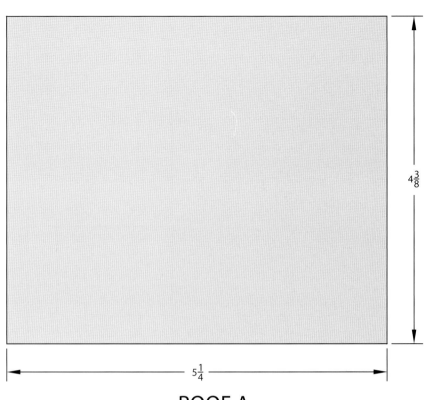

$4\frac{3}{8}$

$5\frac{1}{4}$

ROOF A
5/8" X 4-3/8" X 5-1/4"

5

$5\frac{1}{4}$

ROOF B
5/8" X 5" X 5-1/4"

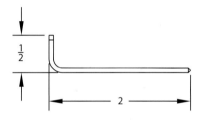

$\frac{1}{2}$

2

FINISHING NAIL
8d X 2-1/2"　(2 REQ'D)

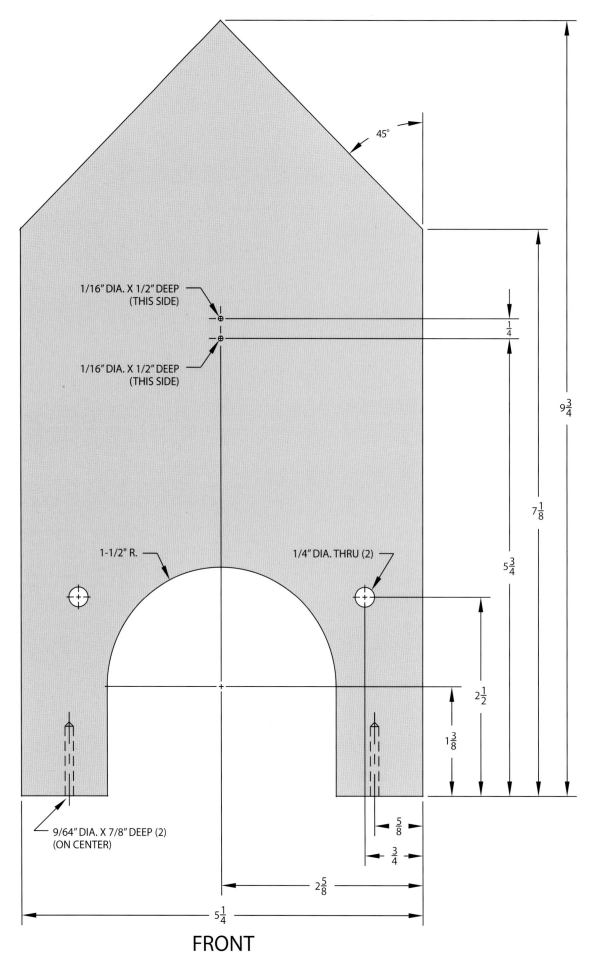

1/16" DIA. X 1/2" DEEP
(THIS SIDE)

1/16" DIA. X 1/2" DEEP
(THIS SIDE)

45°

$9\frac{3}{4}$

$7\frac{1}{8}$

$5\frac{3}{4}$

$\frac{1}{4}$

1-1/2" R.

1/4" DIA. THRU (2)

$2\frac{1}{2}$

$1\frac{3}{8}$

9/64" DIA. X 7/8" DEEP (2)
(ON CENTER)

$\frac{5}{8}$

$\frac{3}{4}$

$2\frac{5}{8}$

$5\frac{1}{4}$

FRONT

5/8" X 5-1/4" X 9-3/4"

1/4″ DIA.

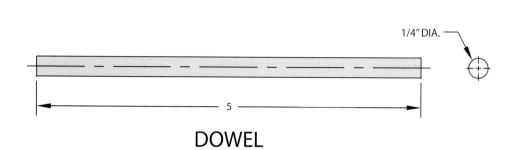

DOWEL
1/4″ DIA. X 5″   (2 REQ'D)

5

2-1/4″ DIA. THRU
(TWO PIECES ONLY)

11/64″ DIA. THRU (2)
C'SINK FOR SCREW
(OTHER SIDE)
(ONE PIECE ONLY)

$5\frac{1}{4}$

$2\frac{5}{8}$

$1\frac{9}{16}$

$\frac{5}{8}$

$1\frac{9}{16}$

$2\frac{5}{8}$

$5\frac{1}{4}$

WELL
5/8″ X 5-1/4″ X 5-1/4″   (5 REQ'D)

Traditional Bird Feeder

This large-capacity bird feeder has a hinged top that makes it easy to fill. The 8" x 10" (203 x 254mm) clear front plate, which lifts out for cleaning, can be plastic or glass.

Standard screen door hooks keep the top piece securely closed, while the slanted roof sheds water. The project is designed to be attached to a vertical surface, like a tree trunk or a vertical wood or metal post.

TIP: If you have an 8" x 10" (203 x 254mm) picture frame you're not using, you can use the glass from that frame for this project.

How-To Instructions

This project is constructed from ¾" (19mm) lumber. It is pictured made from pine, but other species could be used instead. Cedar would be a good choice, because it lasts a long time outdoors, even without wood finish. Assembly is completed with water-resistant glue and either nails or screws as desired. The amount of lumber required is shown in the Cutting Diagram.

The plans show ¼" (6mm) holes in the top and bottom of the Back piece. These holes are used only if mounting the project with wood screws. If mounting on a vertical wood post, use flush-mount hangers.

Begin by cutting each of the parts as described below. Then, assemble the project according to the Final Assembly instructions and as shown in the Assembly Drawing.

TRAY FRONT AND TRAY BOTTOM: Lay out and cut to size from ¾" (19mm) stock.

DOWEL: Lay out and cut to length from ¾" dowel stock.

TRAY SIDE: Lay out and cut to size from ¾" (19mm) stock. Drill the ¾" (19mm)-diameter hole ⅜" (10mm) deep. (One right-hand and one left-hand piece required.)

SIDE: Lay out and cut to size from ¾" (19mm) stock. Cut the groove ⅛" wide x ⁵⁄₁₆" deep (3 x 8mm). (One right-hand and one left-hand piece required.)

LID: Lay out and cut to size from ¾" (19mm) stock. Cut the 30-degree bevel.

BACK: Lay out and cut to size from ¾" (19mm) stock. Drill the ¼" (6mm) mounting holes through.

SANDING: Finish-sand all parts.

FINAL ASSEMBLY

STEP 1: Attach the Tray Front to the Tray Bottom. Attach one Tray Side piece to the Tray Front/Tray Bottom assembly. Be sure the ¾" (19mm)-diameter ⅜" (10mm)-deep hole is in the correct position. Position the dowel and attach the second Side piece. Attach the Tray assembly to the Back where shown. Drive a nail through the edge of one of the Tray Side pieces and into the dowel to keep it from rotating in the hole.

STEP 2: Attach the Side pieces to the Back. Insert the glass or acrylic plate in the ⅛" (3mm) grooves in the Side pieces.

STEP 3: Center the hinges 2½" (64mm) from the edges of the Back piece and use them to attach the Lid to the Back. Attach the screen-door hooks to the bottom of the Lid and Side pieces approximately 2" (51mm) back from the front edge of the Side pieces.

FINISHING: Paint or stain as desired.

TIP: Choose wild food bird mixes wisely. If you have only one feeder, it may seem like a good idea to purchase a mix. Some mixes contain only about 5 percent sunflower seeds. Birds like blue jays, and some wrens, have an annoying habit of throwing out the less desirable seeds in search of the sunflower seeds they favor. Although other birds usually eat the spilled seeds under your feeder, it can be disheartening to see the waste and have to refill more frequently. Once you see which birds come to your feeder, either select the type of seed your favorite birds prefer or, better yet, add additional feeders, each with seeds specific to various species.

Bill of Materials

Qty.	Part	Size of Material
1	Tray Front	¾" x 2" x 8" (19 x 51 x 203mm)
2	Tray Side	¾" x 2" x 7¾" (19 x 51 x 197mm)
1	Tray Bottom	¾" x 5" x 8" (19 x 127 x 203mm)
2	Side	¾" x 7¹⁄₁₆" x 12½" (19 x 179 x 318mm)
1	Lid	¾" x 8¼" x 12½" (19 x 210 x 318mm)
1	Back	¾" x 11" x 17½" (19 x 279 x 445mm)
1	Dowel	¾" (19mm) diameter; 8¾" (222mm) long
1	Acrylic Plate	8" x 10" (203 x 254mm)
1 pair	Hinge w/ Screw	1½" (38mm)
1 pair	Screen-Door Hook	1½" (38mm)
1 pair	Flush-Mount Hanger	1¾" x 1½" (44 x 38mm)

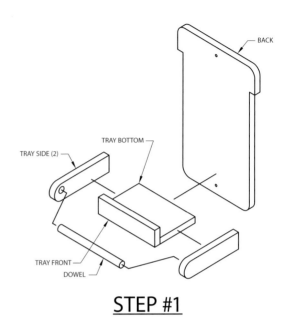

STEP #1

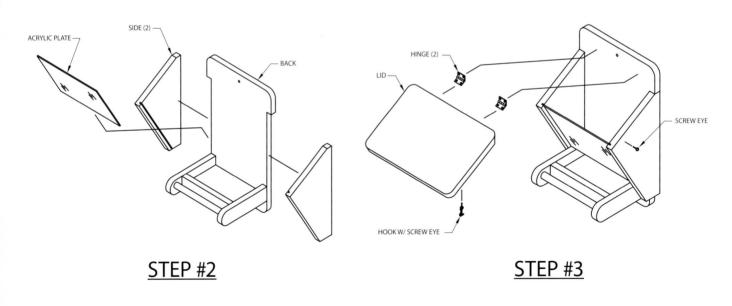

STEP #2

STEP #3

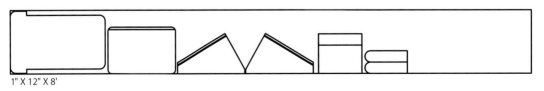

1" X 12" X 8'

CUTTING DIAGRAM

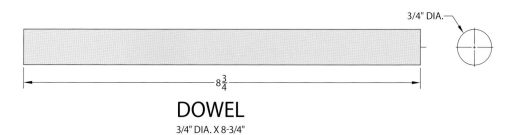

3/4" DIA.

DOWEL
3/4" DIA. X 8-3/4"

$8\frac{3}{4}$

5

8

TRAY BOTTOM
3/4" X 5" X 8"

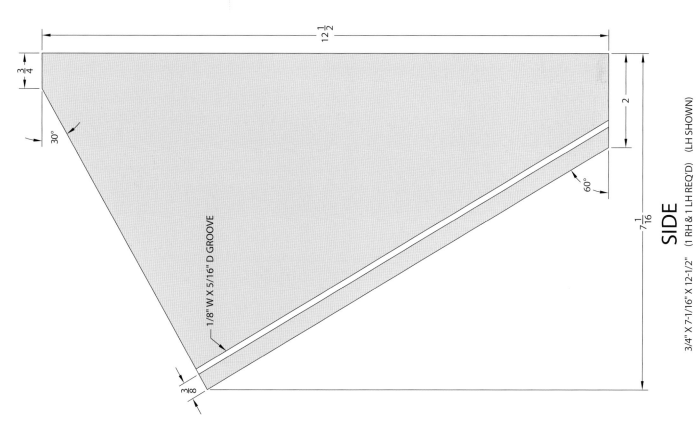

$12\frac{1}{2}$

$\frac{3}{4}$

30°

2

60°

1/8" W X 5/16" D GROOVE

$\frac{3}{8}$

$7\frac{1}{16}$

SIDE

3/4" X 7-1/16" X 12-1/2" (1 RH & 1 LH REQ'D) (LH SHOWN)

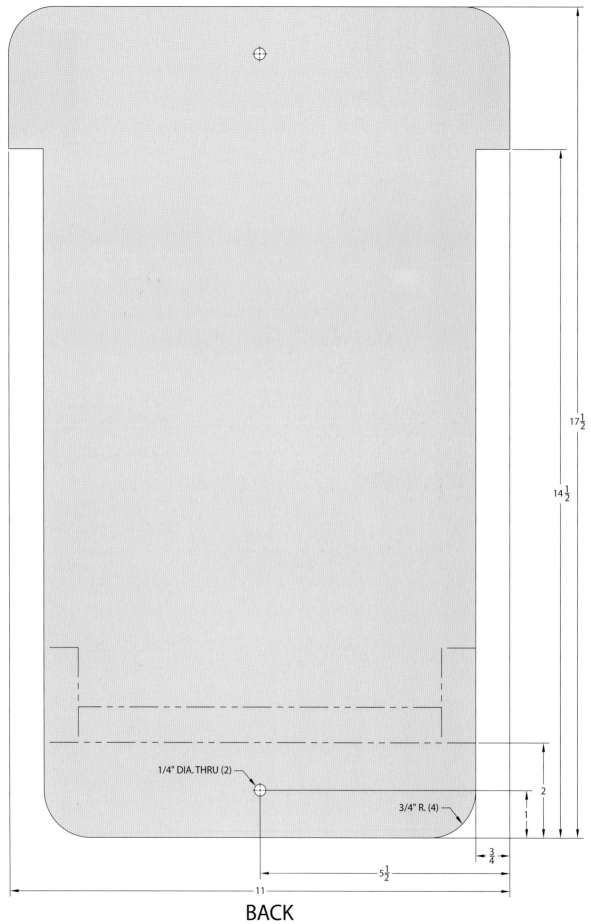

$17\frac{1}{2}$

$14\frac{1}{2}$

1/4" DIA. THRU (2)

3/4" R. (4)

2

1

$\frac{3}{4}$

$5\frac{1}{2}$

11

BACK
3/4" X 11" X 17-1/2"

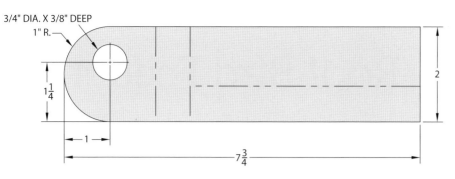

3/4" DIA. X 3/8" DEEP

1" R.

1¼

1

7¾

2

TRAY SIDE
3/4" X 2" X 7-3/4"   (1 RH & 1 LH REQ'D)   (LH SHOWN)

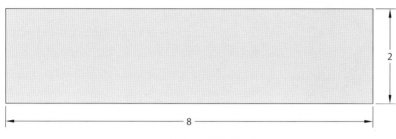

2

8

TRAY FRONT
3/4" X 2" X 8"

30°

8¼

3/4" R. (4)

12½

¾

LID
3/4" X 8-1/4" X 12-1/2"

Scallop-Roof Bird Feeder

This bird feeder includes the most important features a hanging feeder should have. The roof lifts straight up, making the feeder fast and convenient to refill. Birds can access the food from two sides, reducing competition. Clear plastic side plates are easily removable for cleaning and let you keep an eye on the level of seed.

Small squares of wood with beveled ends inside the feeder partially cover the feed holes, a simple technique that prevents seed from spilling out of the feeder. This innovative feature works just as well as the specialized metal baffles found on some mass-produced bird feeders. The main difference is this design costs less, is more natural for the birds, and is more environmentally friendly to manufacture.

The attractive scalloped shingles are for decoration only. You can omit the shingles to speed the building process with no negative result on the utility or effectiveness of the project.

How-To Instructions

This project is constructed primarily from ¾" (19mm) lumber. It is pictured in pine, but cedar and redwood both stand up well outdoors and are excellent alternatives.

The Brace piece and Spreader piece are both thicker than ¾" (19mm) and require that you glue pieces of ¾" (19mm) lumber together and then cut the parts to size and shape. Cut the grooves in the Side pieces using a table saw. The width of these grooves can be less than the ⅛" (3mm) width specified, as long as the clear acrylic plastic plate can slide in them.

Plans are not provided for the Roof A and Roof B pieces. These are simple rectangular parts. Cut them to the width and length called for in the Bill of Materials.

Plans are provided for the optional scallop-shaped shingles should you decide to add them to the roof. Use thin exterior-grade plywood to make the shingles.

Begin by cutting each of the parts as described below. Then, assemble the project according to the Final Assembly instructions and as shown in the Assembly Drawing.

TIP: The best time to feed birds is in winter or when severe weather restricts the amount of available seed or insects. In northern climates, start feeding birds before the onset of cold weather. Although food becomes more readily available to birds in the spring and summer, they will appreciate fruits and nectar that may be harder for them to find in nature.

SPACER: Lay out and cut to size from ⁵⁄₃₂" (4mm) plywood. (Two pieces required.)

SHINGLE A AND SHINGLE B: Lay out and cut to size from ⁵⁄₃₂" (4mm) plywood.

SHINGLE C: Lay out and cut to size from ⁵⁄₃₂" (4mm) plywood. (Six pieces required.)

SHINGLE D: Lay out and cut to size from ⁵⁄₃₂" (4mm) plywood. (Eight pieces required.)

SHIELD: Lay out and cut to size from ¾" (19mm) stock. Cut the 45-degree bevels. (Four pieces required.)

ROOF A AND ROOF B: Lay out and cut to size from ¾" (19mm) stock according to the dimensions given in the Bill of Materials.

SIDE: Lay out and cut to size from ¾" (19mm) stock. Cut the ⅛"-wide-by-¼"-deep (3 by 6mm) grooves. Drill the ⅜" (10mm)-diameter holes ⅝" (16mm) deep. Drill or saw the 2¼" (57mm)-diameter holes. (Two pieces required.)

BASE: Lay out and cut to size from ¾" (19mm) stock. Drill the ⁹⁄₆₄" (3.6 mm)-diameter screw clearance holes through and countersink for screws.

BRACE: Lay out and cut to size from 1½" (38mm) stock. Drill the ⅜" (10mm)-diameter hole through after assembly.

SPREADER: Lay out and cut three pieces of ¾" (19mm) stock to size and glue up to form a 2¼" (57mm)-thick block. Cut the bevels to form the Spreader piece.

DOWEL: Lay out and cut to length from ⅜" (10mm) dowel stock. (Four pieces required.)

ACRYLIC PLATE: Lay out and cut the ⅜" (10mm) radii. (Two pieces required.)

SANDING: Finish-sand all parts.

FINAL ASSEMBLY

STEP 1: Glue the Shield pieces to the Side piece where shown. Glue the dowels in the ⅜" (10mm) holes.

STEP 2: Attach the Side pieces to the Base with the 1¾" (44mm) screws. Glue and nail the Brace and Spreader between the Side pieces where shown.

STEP 3: Insert the acrylic plates into the saw grooves in the Side pieces. Attach the Roof A and Roof B pieces to each other. To hang the finished project, drill a ⅜" (10mm)-diameter hole through the center of the peak of the Roof and Brace (after attaching the shingles in Step 4). Pass a length of ¼" (6mm) rope though the hole and knot the end to secure. This will allow for the Roof to be raised up for refilling.

STEP 4: Glue the Spacers to the Roof pieces. If adding the shingles, mark a line across the Roof pieces 1¼" (32mm) from the end as shown. Mark five more lines at ⅞" (22mm) intervals starting from the 1¼" (32mm) line. Glue and nail the Shingle D pieces in place using the 1¼" (32mm) guidelines. Glue and nail a Shingle C piece in place on each side using the ⅞" (22mm) guidelines so they overlap the Shingle D pieces. Repeat the process, alternating the Shingle B and Shingle C pieces, until the peak of the Roof is reached. Glue and nail the Shingle A and Shingle B pieces in place for a cap.

FINISHING: All parts were finished with sanding sealer and polyurethane. Paint the exposed parts of the roof and the underside of the overhanging shingles white. Paint the top surface and edges of the shingles copper. Cover the painted parts with a top coat of Delta Clear Exterior Varnish.

Bill of Materials

Qty.	Part	Size of Material
2	Spacer	⁵⁄₃₂" x ½" x 8½" (4 x 13 x 216mm)
1	Shingle A	⁵⁄₃₂" x 1" x 9" (4 x 25 x 229mm)
1	Shingle B	⁵⁄₃₂" x 1⅛" x 9" (4 x 29 x 229mm)
6	Shingle C	⁵⁄₃₂" x 1¾" x 9" (4 x 22 x 229mm)
8	Shingle D	⁵⁄₃₂" x 1¾" x 9" (4 x 22 x 229mm)
4	Shield	¾" x 3⅜" x 3¾" (19 x 86 x 95mm)
1	Roof A	¾" x 5¾" x 8½" (19 x 146 x 216mm) (not drawn)
1	Roof B	¾" x 6½" x 8½" (19 x 165 x 216mm) (not drawn)
2	Side	¾" x 6½" x 13⅞" (19 x 165 x 352mm)
1	Base	¾" x 10½" x 10½" (19 x 267 x 267mm)
1	Brace	1¼" x 1¼" x 5" (32 x 32 x 127mm)
1	Spreader	2¼" x 5" x 5½" (57 x 127 x 140mm)
4	Dowel	⅜" (10mm) diameter; 2¾" (70mm) long
2	Acrylic Plate	¹⁄₁₀" x 5⅜" x 11" (2.5 x 137 x 279mm)
6	#6 Flat-Head Screw	1¾" (44mm)

Paints and Stains

Qty.	Generic Color	Part Number
1	Copper	2 oz. (57 g.)
1	White	2 oz. (57 g.)
1	Exterior Varnish, Stain	8 oz. (227 g.)

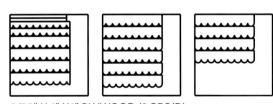

5/32" X 1" X1" PLYWOOD (3 REQ'D)

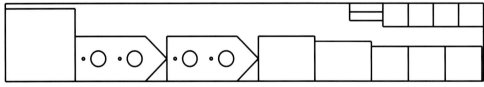

1" X 12" X 6'

CUTTING DIAGRAM

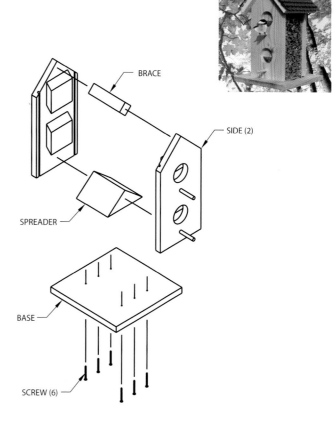

DRILL 3/8" HOLE
THRU ROOF & BRACE

BRACE

SIDE (2)

SPREADER

BASE

SCREW (6)

STEP #2

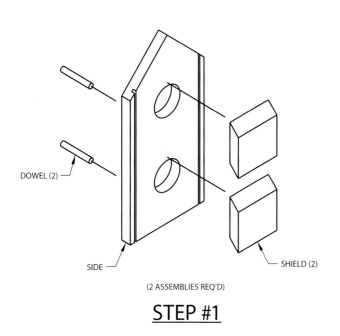

DOWEL (2)

SIDE

SHIELD (2)

(2 ASSEMBLIES REQ'D)

STEP #1

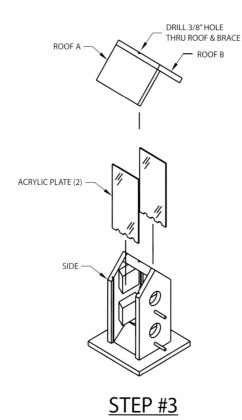

ROOF A

ROOF B

ACRYLIC PLATE (2)

SIDE

STEP #3

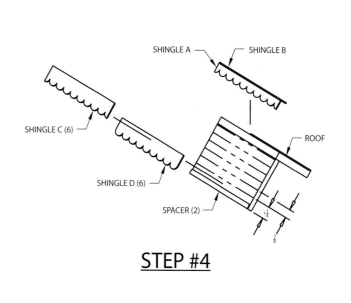

SHINGLE A

SHINGLE B

SHINGLE C (6)

SHINGLE D (6)

SPACER (2)

ROOF

STEP #4

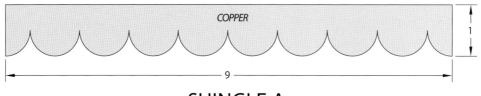

SHINGLE A
5/32" X 1" X 9"

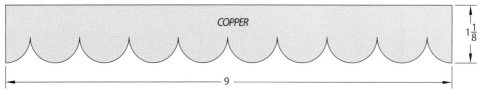

SHINGLE B
5/32" X 1-1/8" X 9"

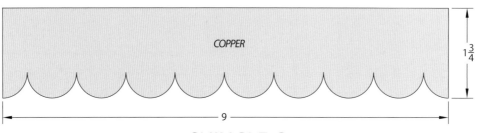

SHINGLE C
5/32" X 1-3/4" X 9"   (6 REQ'D)

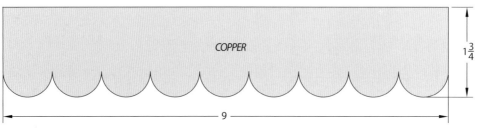

SHINGLE D
5/32" X 1-3/4" X 9"   (8 REQ'D)

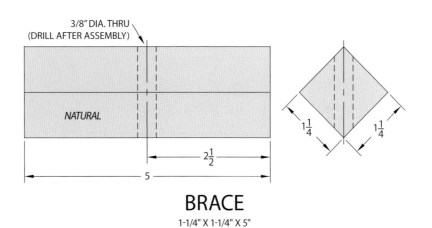

BRACE
1-1/4" X 1-1/4" X 5"

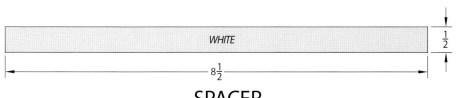

SPACER
5/32" X 1/2" X 8-1/2"   (2 REQ'D)

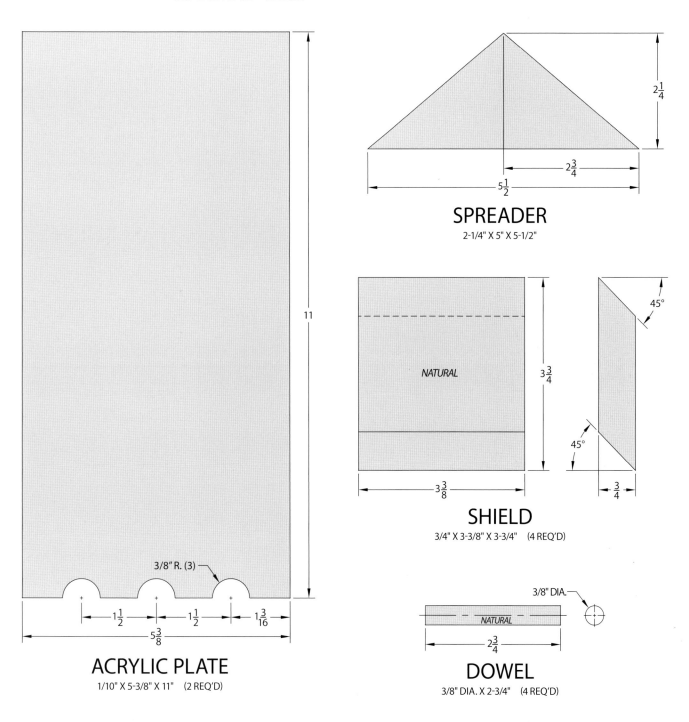

SPREADER
2-1/4" X 5" X 5-1/2"

SHIELD
3/4" X 3-3/8" X 3-3/4"   (4 REQ'D)

ACRYLIC PLATE
1/10" X 5-3/8" X 11"   (2 REQ'D)

3/8" R. (3)

DOWEL
3/8" DIA. X 2-3/4"   (4 REQ'D)

TIP: Be sure to place feeders in open areas where squirrels can't rob your seed, but close to bushes and other appropriate cover. Trees and shrubs offer birds protection from ice, rain, snow, winter wind, and hot sun. Such shelter also helps prevent attacks from hawks and other predators.

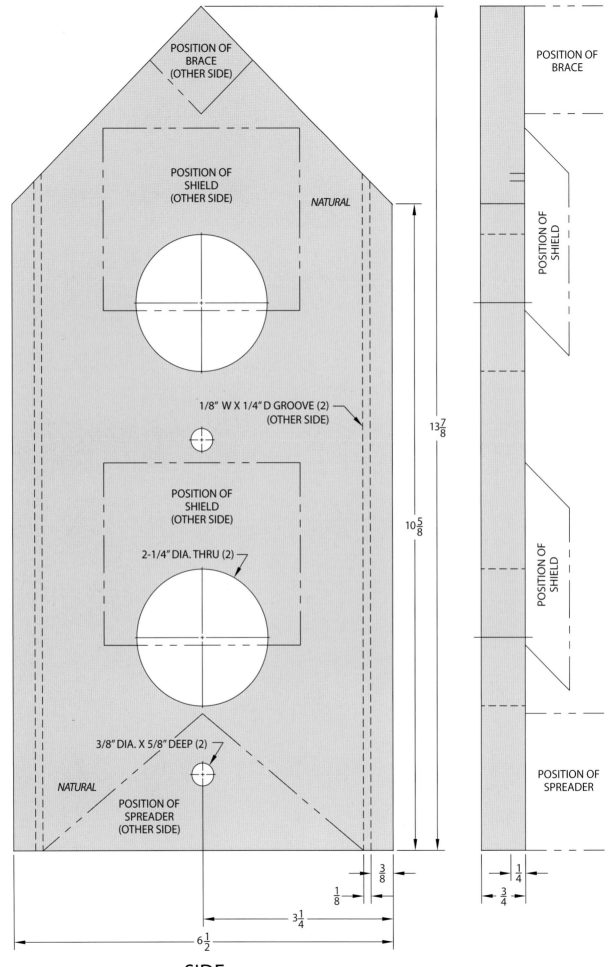

POSITION OF
BRACE
(OTHER SIDE)

POSITION OF
BRACE

POSITION OF
SHIELD
(OTHER SIDE)

NATURAL

POSITION OF
SHIELD

1/8" W X 1/4" D GROOVE (2)
(OTHER SIDE)

$13\frac{7}{8}$

$10\frac{5}{8}$

POSITION OF
SHIELD
(OTHER SIDE)

2-1/4" DIA. THRU (2)

POSITION OF
SHIELD

3/8" DIA. X 5/8" DEEP (2)

NATURAL

POSITION OF
SPREADER
(OTHER SIDE)

POSITION OF
SPREADER

$\frac{3}{8}$

$\frac{1}{8}$

$\frac{1}{4}$

$\frac{3}{4}$

$3\frac{1}{4}$

$6\frac{1}{2}$

SIDE
3/4" X 6-1/2" X 13-7/8"   (2 REQ'D)

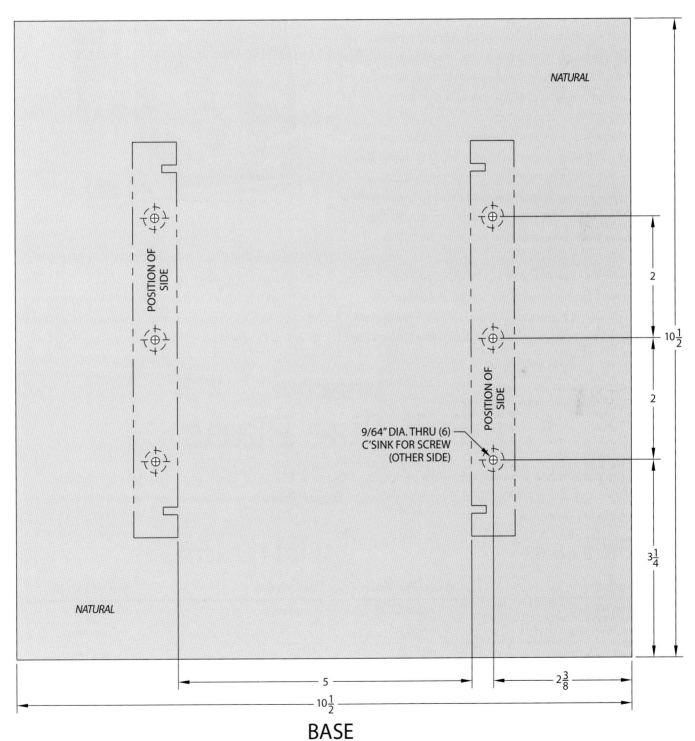

NATURAL

POSITION OF
SIDE

POSITION OF
SIDE

9/64" DIA. THRU (6)
C'SINK FOR SCREW
(OTHER SIDE)

2

$10\frac{1}{2}$

2

$3\frac{1}{4}$

NATURAL

5

$2\frac{3}{8}$

$10\frac{1}{2}$

BASE
3/4" X 10-1/2" X 10-1/2"

About the Author

Paul Meisel began designing projects as an industrial arts instructor, recognizing beginning students' need for exciting projects that do not exceed their skill level.

He and his wife then began a mail-order company to distribute well-designed plans and hard-to-find specialty hardware parts to classrooms and hobbyist woodworkers. Meisel Hardware Specialties is now a leading project plan and woodworking supply company; all of its more than 3,500 woodworking projects meet his rigid criteria for simple, practical construction.

Meisel's clean, straightforward designs feature fresh ideas and create maximum impact, using common lumber sizes and simple painting and finishing techniques. He specifies readily available materials and power tools.

Meisel's designs have received numerous awards and appeared in publications including *Scroll Saw Woodworking and Crafts*.

In 1993, Meisel wrote *Country Mailboxes* with Patrick Spielman. His books with Fox Chapel Publishing are *Making Lawn Ornaments in Wood* (1999), *The Big Book of Christmas Scroll Saw Projects* (2002), *The How-to Book* of *Birdhouses and Bird Feeders* (2004), and *Wild & Wacky Birdhouses and Feeders* (2012).

Meisel has a backyard nesting and feeding station at his suburban Minneapolis home. A member of a Bluebird Recovery Program, he maintains his own bluebird trail.

APPENDIX A:
Full-Size Plans

Full-size pattern sheets can be ordered for each of the projects in this book. Order plans from Meisel Hardware Specialties by calling 1-800-441-9870 or visiting *www.meiselwoodhobby.com*. Be sure to use the part number below when placing your order.

Birdhouses

Description	Meisel Part No.
Martin House	#W2448
Bluebird House	#W3025
Wood Duck House	#W3107
Window View Birdhouse	#W3152
Chickadee Birdhouse and Roost	#W3450
Small Raptor Nest Box	#W3581

Bird Feeders

Description	Meisel Part No.
Suet Feeder	#W3235
Squirrel-Proof Bird Feeder	#W3284
Oriole Wishing Well Feeder	#W3420
Traditional Bird Feeder	#W3462
Underside Suet Feeder	#W3466
Scallop-Roof Feeder	#W3482

APPENDIX B:
Additional Resources

The following resources are recommended by the author:

The Bird's Paradise
20785 Morris Rd.
Conneautville, PA 16406
(800) 872-0103

This company is a good source for bluebird houses, aluminum perching arms, purple martin gourd houses and poles, martin apartments, winch operated collapsible mounting poles, predator guards, and devices to discourage sparrows. Mail order catalog available.

Minnesota Waterfowl Association— Prairie Pothole Chapter
www.prairiepotholeday.com

The Prairie Pothole Chapter of the Minnesota Waterfowl Association has been building and maintaining wood duck nesting boxes for more than 28 years. The chapter provides education and raises money to promote habitat projects. They offer predator guards for sale to the public to help raise funds. For information click on Wood Duck Boxes and Guards on the home page of their web site.

The National Audubon Society
225 Varick Street
New York, NY 10014
(212) 979-3000
www.audubon.org

The mission of the Audubon Society is to conserve and restore natural ecosystems, focusing on birds, other wildlife, and their habitats for the benefit of humanity and the earth's biological diversity. They have nearly five hundred chapters nationwide.

National Bird Feeding Society
Millikin University
1184 W. Main Street
Decatur, IL 62522
(866) 945-3247
www.birdfeeding.org

The National Bird Feeding Society helps make backyard bird feeding and bird watching better—for people and birds. It accomplishes this mission by connecting hobbyists with education and research about backyard bird feeding.

North American Bluebird Society
P.O. Box 244
Wilmot, OH 44689-0244
(330) 359-5511
www.nabluebirdsociety.org

The North American Bluebird Society is a non-profit education, conservation, and research organization that promotes the recovery of bluebirds and other native cavity-nesting bird species in North America.

The Purple Martin Conservation Association
301 Peninsula Dr. Suite 6
Erie, PA 16505
(814) 833-7656
www.purplemartin.org

The Purple Martin Conservation Association is a nonprofit organization dedicated to the conservation of purple martins through scientific research, state of the art management techniques, and public education, with the goal of increasing martin populations throughout North America.

The Wood Duck Society
www.woodducksociety.com

The Wood Duck Society is a group of wood duck enthusiasts led by volunteer directors who have lifetime wood duck and wildlife expertise and who enjoy sharing their knowledge and experiences with others.

APPENDIX C:
Nest Box Dimensions

Dimensions are in inches (and millimeters) unless otherwise noted.

Species		Floor Size	Entry Hole (A)	Hole above Floor (B)	Distance from Ground (C)
	American Kestrel	8" x 9" (203 x 229mm)	3" (76mm)	8"–10" (203–254mm)	10'–30' (3048–9144mm)
	American Robin	5" x 8" (127 x 203mm)	Open sides	—	8'–10' (2438–3048mm)
	Bluebird	3½" x 3½" (89 x 89mm)	1⅜" x 2¼" (35 x 57mm)	5"–7" (127–178mm)	5'–7' (1524–2134mm)
	Boreal Owl	8" x 9" (203 x 229mm)	3" (76mm)	8"–10" (203–254mm)	16'–20' (4877–6069mm)
	Chickadee	4" x 4" (102 x 102mm)	1⅛" (29mm)	6"–8" (152–203mm)	5'–15' (1524–4572mm)
	Finches	6" x 6" (152 x 152mm)	2" (51mm)	4"–6" (102–152mm)	8'–12' (2438–3658mm)
	Flycatcher	6" x 6" (152 x 152mm)	1¾"–2" (44–51mm)	6"–8" (152–203mm)	5'–15' (1524–4572mm)
	Northern Screech Owl	8" x 9" (203–229mm)	3" (76mm)	8"–10" (203–254mm)	10' (3048mm)
	Northern Saw-Whet Owl	8" x 9" (203–229mm)	3" (76mm)	8"–10" (203–254mm)	14' (4267mm)

A

B

C

Species	Floor Size	Entry Hole (A)	Hole above Floor (B)	Distance from Ground (C)
Nuthatch	4" x 4" (102 x 102mm)	1¼" (32mm)	6"–8" (152–203mm)	5'–15' (1524–4572mm)
Phoebe	5" x 8" (127–203mm)	Open sides	—	8'–12' (2438–3658mm)
Purple Martin	6" x 6" (152 x 152mm)	2" (51mm)	1" (25mm)	8'–18' (2438–5486mm)
Sparrow	5" x 5" (127 x 127mm)	1½" (38mm)	4"–8" (102–203mm)	4'–12' (1219–3658mm)
Barn Swallow	5" x 5" (127 x 127mm)	Open sides	—	8'–12' (2438–3658mm)
Tree Swallow	5" x 5" (127 x 127mm)	1½" (38mm)	2"–5" (51–127mm)	10'–15' (3048–4572mm)
Titmouse	4" x 4" (102 x 102mm)	1¼" (32mm)	6"–8" (152–203mm)	6'–15' (1829–4572mm)
Warbler	4" x 4" (102 x 102mm)	1½" (38mm)	5" (127mm)	4'–7' (1219–2134mm)
Wrens	4" x 4" (102 x 102mm)	1"–1¼" (25–32mm)	3"–6" (76–152mm)	6'–10' (1829–3048mm)

APPENDIX D:
Feeding Preferences

East

Legend: ● = Most Preferred, ○ = Preferred

PERCHING BIRDS

BIRDS	Oil Sunflower	Hulled Sunflower	Striped Sunflower	Millet	Nyjer® (Thistle)	Cracked Corn	In-Shell Peanuts	Shelled Peanuts	Suet	Safflower	Mealworms	Fruit	Nectar*
Bluebirds											●		
Cardinal, Northern	●	○	○							○			
Chickadees	●	○						○			○		
Finch, House	●	●		○	○								
Finch, Purple	●	○											
Goldfinches	○	●	○		●								
Grosbeaks	●	○	○								●		
Hummingbirds													●
Jays			○				●	○					
Nuthatches	●	○						○	●				
Orioles											○	●	●
Siskin, Pine	○	●	○		●								
Titmouse, Tufted								●	●				
Woodpeckers		○						○	●				
Wrens										○	●		

GROUND FEEDING BIRDS

BIRDS	Oil Sunflower	Hulled Sunflower	Striped Sunflower	Millet	Nyjer® (Thistle)	Cracked Corn	In-Shell Peanuts	Shelled Peanuts	Suet	Safflower	Mealworms	Fruit	Nectar*
Dove, Mourning	●	○		●		○				○			
Juncos	○	○		●		○							
Sparrow, House	○	○		●		○							
Sparrows, Native				●						○			
Towhees	○			●		○					●		

* Our own Pure Hummer Sugar™

* Nyjer® is a registered trademark of the Wild Bird Feeding Industry

Courtesy of Wild Bird Centers of America, Inc.

■ **Most Preferred**   ■ **Preferred**

West

BIRDS		Oil Sunflower	Striped Sunflower	Hulled Sunflower	Millet	Safflower	Nyjer® (Thistle)	Cracked Corn	In-Shell Peanuts	Shelled Peanuts	Suet	Mealworms	Fruit	Nectar*
PERCHING BIRDS	Bluebirds											Most Preferred		
	Bushtit	Preferred		Preferred					Most Preferred	Preferred	Most Preferred			
	Chickadees	Most Preferred	Preferred	Preferred							Most Preferred	Preferred		
	Finches	Most Preferred	Most Preferred	Preferred										
	Flickers	Preferred	Preferred	Preferred						Preferred	Most Preferred			
	Goldfinches	Most Preferred		Most Preferred			Most Preferred							
	Grosbeaks	Most Preferred	Most Preferred	Most Preferred										
	Hummingbirds													Most Preferred
	Jays	Preferred							Most Preferred	Most Preferred	Preferred	Preferred		
	Kinglets			Preferred							Most Preferred			
	Nuthatches	Most Preferred	Preferred	Preferred						Most Preferred	Most Preferred			
	Orioles												Most Preferred	Most Preferred
	Siskin, Pine	Preferred		Most Preferred			Most Preferred							
	Titmouse	Most Preferred	Preferred	Preferred		Preferred				Preferred	Most Preferred			
	Woodpeckers	Most Preferred								Most Preferred	Most Preferred		Preferred	
	Wrens									Preferred	Preferred	Most Preferred		
GROUND FEEDING BIRDS	Dove, Mourning	Preferred		Preferred	Most Preferred			Preferred						
	Juncos	Preferred		Preferred	Most Preferred			Most Preferred						
	Sparrows, Native	Preferred		Preferred	Most Preferred			Preferred						
	Towhees				Most Preferred			Preferred						

* Our own Pure Hummer Sugar™

* Nyjer® is a registered trademark of the Wild Bird Feeding Industry

Courtesy of Wild Bird Centers of America, Inc.

■ **Most Preferred** ■ **Preferred**

Index

YEARBOOK

Catalog #32
$2.00

MEISEL
HARDWARE SPECIALTIES

The Most Trusted Name in Woodworking Plans

Plans for over 1,000 Woodworking Projects!

Pg. 2

Pg. 50

Pg. 59

Pg. 14

Pg. 34

Pg. 7

August
2011
to
July
2012

Order Online & SAVE 10%!

HUGE Specialty Hardware Selection Available!

Credit Card Customers Call Toll Free

1-800-441-9870

www.meiselwoodhobby.com

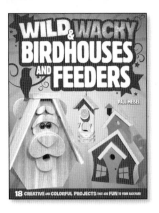

Wild & Wacky Birdhouses and Feeders

18 Creative and Colorful Projects That Add Fun to Your Backyard
By Paul Meisel

Whether it's the birdhouse cleverly designed to look like a security camera, or the player piano squirrel feeder that will turn your resident animals into musicians, readers are sure to find a project that will delight and amuse.

ISBN: 978-1-56523-679-0
$19.95 · 152 Pages

Tree Craft

35 Rustic Wood Projects That Bring the Outdoors In
By Chris Lubkemann

Beautify your home with rustic accents made from twigs and branches. More than 35 eco-chic projects for a coat rack, curtain rods, candle holders, desk sets, picture frames, a table, chess set, and more.

ISBN: 978-1-56523-455-0
$19.95 · 128 Pages

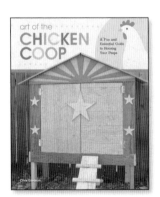

Making Lawn Ornaments In Wood

Complete Building Techniques and Patterns
By Paul Meisel

New edition with 16 pages of new patterns, including 20 ready to use full-size patterns.

ISBN: 978-1-56523-104-7
$14.95 · 136 Pages

Outdoor Furniture (Built to Last)

14 Timeless Woodworking Projects for the Yard, Deck, and Patio
By Skills Institute Press, Editor, John Kelsey

Design and build beautiful wooden outdoor furniture sturdy enough to withstand Mother Nature with the detailed techniques and step by step instructions in this handy guide.

ISBN: 978-1-56523-500-7
$19.95 · 144 Pages

Art of the Chicken Coop

A Fun and Essential Guide to Housing Your Peeps
By Chris Gleason

A fresh approach to designing and building chicken coops with seven stylish designs that your flock will adore and your neighbors will envy.

ISBN: 978-1-56523-542-7
$19.95 · 160 Pages

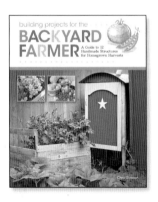

Building Projects for the Backyard Farmer

A Guide to 21 Handmade Structures for Homegrown Harvests
By Chris Gleason

With this book, homeowners will obtain both inspiration and instruction for transforming their grassy yard into a lush farm that can produce all the food they need.

ISBN: 978-1-56523-543-4
$19.95 · 144 Pages